natural self discovery

A creative journey to sanity
in an increasingly insane world

"Insanity is doing the same thing over and over again and expecting different results."

~Albert Einstein

Natural Self Discovery

Published by Natural Brand Studios, SPC

Available on Amazon or at

www.pamelahoke.com

just pause
©2024, pamela hoke

Feather as Metaphor

A feather is truly a gift.
It serves as our reminder to pause and assess our relationship
with our life source, ourselves and others.

Feathers remind us of our innate love and yearning for nature.
Feathers represent the intelligent balance of the natural world.

Feathers can serve as a way to remind us to lighten up
when things are getting heavy, to re-balance.
Things are feeling heavy right now.
We have become heavy on ourselves and each other
because of the unfair weight we are placing upon Earth, the
sustaining source of our existence.

We feel lonely because we have become a lonely species,
separated from our actual "real" world
because we remain in our human-centric story world.
We deeply miss and yearn for our kinship with our life source.

Earth, in it's brilliant design to sustain all of life,
is signaling to us it's time to re-write our human-centric stories
to restore our kinship with the natural world.

Our dominant societal thinking has severed this primal kinship,
and has led to an imbalanced heaviness of mind, body and
spirit of our human family.

Feathers can represent that much needed pause,
to seek sanity from the insanity created by our stories.

We can learn to pause long enough to let in the expansive lens
of the "real" world beyond our limited human-centric lens.

The sooner we learn to regularly take pause
to value our innate sensory awareness and creative intelligence,
the sooner we can restore a balanced relationship within
ourselves, so we can thrive in solutions
rather than perpetuating problems,
we can how to effectively lead ourselves
in alignment with our life source, and each other.

Creating a habit of including a simple feather, or any being from nature into our daily human story lens creates space for this ancient natural intelligence to guide us into our next frontier of maturity as a species.

I hope you might allow yourself the gift of pause with nature,
and enter this realm of natural self discovery with me.

We can re-set our human story, starting with our own,
We can re-learn how to value and trust the process of
transformation through creative discovery with nature
as vital to our existence and purpose.

Let's learn to travel our shared human experience
a little lighter...
on ourselves,
on each other,
and our planet.

May we lighten up with love, Pam

For Alex, Angela. Love, Mom

For my fellow human travelers who sense there is a way to travel lighter on our shared planet. Here's to transforming with new eyes and wings!

This book would not be possible without the amazing fellow humans that have graced me with their moments and energy throughout our time walking this planet together.

Whether a colleague, community connection, client, boss, teacher, leader, motivational speaker or author, I have received the inspiration, courage and strength from each of you, and I am eternally grateful.

Thank you, Mother Earth, for being our life source and the ultimate teacher of sustainability, transformation and regenerative processes

Thank you to my close family and friends who have embraced my deep love for expressing nature's gifts and helping others over my decades here on the planet with art and design. Also, I am extremely grateful for your encouragement and compassionate patience through the murkiest waters.

To The Ohio State University, thank you for accepting my individualized degree honoring my need to balance both business and art. To the incredible faculty and staff of Evan's School of Public Policy and Social Governance, University of Washington for accepting my proposal and guiding me as I embarked upon the leadership journey of a lifetime.

I have learned so much from all of you, and look forward to learning so much more through our human journey on our shared planet.

TABLE OF CONTENTS

The Serendipity of Adversity ~ *P. Hoke*

I painted this just as I was emerging from my breast cancer treatment. It helps me embrace during difficulty the phrase "no mud, no lotus.

Why did I do this?

A ten year old girl strolled briskly down the curvy road from a cabin in Pymatuning State Park in Ohio. Her grandparents rented two cabins for their annual family summer gathering. She couldn't wait to visit her friends, and get to observe and feel the exuberant energy and love from their enchanting community. It was a massive, artfully constructed, secure, structural weaving of wood that beamed kinship of a deeply connected community working harmoniously together. She loved how this community rippled outward to add vibrant life to the environment and other species around it. To her, it was a wonderland of connection, inspiration and learning. This creative, busy beaver community revealed to her what love is. Visiting this beaver dam community was her ritual. It was her special "sit spot" to escape the bullying at school, to forget for a while about being a latchkey kid of divorce in the 70's, forget her struggles to fit in and be accepted...to just "be." Here, with the creative natural world, she always knew she could just "be."

Excited to see her friends again, she turned onto the natural path that lead her to this beautiful community, yet she could sense something was "off." She couldn't hear the soothing sounds of the water filtering through the dam, the shuffling noises of the busy family members taking care of each other. The pit of her stomach started to feel sick, knowing what she was about to discover. Gone. Vanished. All of it. The beautiful structure and the thriving loving family were gone. Where there once was a vibrant symphony of harmonious life, with clear moving water, there was now stillness. She looked at the murky, shallow, now void-of-life stream. With heart broken, eyes weeping, she just sat there. Her grief led her to start rocking back and forth, full knowing she was in this grieving alone. It was just one of many similar atrocities she had already witnessed in her short 10 years on the planet. Another scenario where the adults would simply justify unfairness to the natural world, justify the violence against natural beings, and even other humans in the name of "progress," void of empathy. She knew there was no one to talk to about this, at least not without the shaming consequences if she pushed the subject. Nope, she would be grieving alone again, and feeling so confused about why.

I always reflect back to that 10 year old girl whenever I need a reminder as to why I have embarked upon such a non-traditional career path throughout my life. Especially knowing that I was passionate about the importance of two areas of study which are still devalued, minimized, commercialized and even tokenized within our industrial society: art and nature. I knew I was an artist, yet I also knew I was a teacher, and I naturally loved solving big puzzles and creating processes. I became fascinated with how both the natural world and business worlds operated, and at the time did not realize that my "whole-picture" lens was not how everyone experienced the world. Somewhere in there I sensed there was a way to balance art and nature within a business-minded society, and refused to become the "starving artist" or "hippie tree-hugger" story.

I knew there was a solution to the societal mis-alignment from nature and creativity, yet could never really put my finger on it. I appreciated the process of businesses, just as I appreciated the process of creating art while enjoying my deep connection with the natural world. I learned how brilliantly nature operated from the abundance of access to nature I got to have, along with my gardening education from my grandmother. I loved fishing, camping and building forts. Thanks to Bob Ross on PBS after school, I was able to experience an early realization of my passion for art and desired to master my natural creative skills, as they became my escape, my outlet, to communicate the need to be in kinship with nature. Bob Ross was way ahead of his time. Art and nature were his therapy from the Viet Nam War, and he shared it with the world. What our business-minded world did to him is what shows clearly the devaluation, minimization, commercialization and tokenization of the arts and the natural world. It is a tragedy that even his own natural born son does not receive profits, nor can even use his own father's name while continuing the legacy of a beautiful nature connected art process. Moving forward after the confusing transition we all experience through teen years, I went onto to propose to The Ohio State University an individualized degree, so I could combine my deep interests in business, nature, and writing with a fine arts major in painting. This led to me entering the most epic adventure in experiential life education: entering the business world while becoming a young mother and wife. I was both exhibiting in galleries while immersed in the world of fashion retail branding in my twenties. I learned everything about corporate presentation, the full cycle of retail branding, and display design, right along with stumbling through the learning the adaptive skills of motherhood and marriage.

Eventually, I sensed the imbalance with the natural world and the unrealistic image of women being created in the fashion world. I had to follow my internal values and purpose and left the corporate retail experience. My young marriage wasn't working out either, so I moved myself, my young son, golden retriever and a bunny rabbit to Florida and received an amazing opportunity to teach art while learning the business world of marketing my own art. After several years, my romantic nature led me back to my ex-husband, and the gift a daughter. This also came with the next career frontier. I founded a boutique brand design business so I could work from home to raise my two children, and put my brand knowledge and design skills to help other entrepreneurial minds succeed. I look back now and wonder how I was able to sustain making these transitions as a young parent, while deeply in love with a man who sadly struggled with addiction to drugs and alcohol his entire life. I can confidently say, beyond the anchor of the deep maternal drive nature instills, it is also because of my tenacity (busy creative beaver traits) with the gift of learning my purpose early through a deep connection with nature and creativity that always kept me going. Amidst the bizarre life challenges, health scares and losses over the years (including recently watching the slow progression of drugs and alcohol take the life of the man who had my heart for over 30 years and raised children with me), my now grown son and daughter and I have managed to come out on the other side fairly whole, healthy and thriving.

I do believe my tenacity to overcome and thrive from life's challenges is because I preserved two things, and did my best, yet not always well, to model it to my adult children: 1. I highly valued maintaining a deep sensory connection with nature as my life source, and 2. I maintained a deep passion for the creative process and maintained my drive to somehow share this with others. It is these two things, as I learned over my over five decades on this planet and the way our systems and mindsets have, and still operate, can feel nearly impossible to sustain.

The book you are now reading is take two. The first take was in 2013. It was received well, a good review article in my local paper in Florida, and sold many copies during a summer residency in Washington. I sensed, however, based on the obvious dominant societal norm of silencing "inconvenient truths" to the system, it would need more work if the critical connection it was meant to make would even be noticed, and it's urgent connection as a solution, possibly be considered .

More truth was revealed that I had much more work to do within myself became abundantly clear after I was delivered my "forced pause" from life. I learned at the age of 45 that I had stage 2 breast cancer. My daughter, late husband and I just moved to the gorgeous island of San Juan in the state of Washington from being offered an incredible artist residency opportunity. My son and his wife were living in Germany, my Mom way over in Florida, and sister in Colorado, and my Dad in Pennsylvania. It was the oddest feeling to realize how separated our family was geographically, yet thanks to technology, we were able to ride through it together.

I was very fortunate to have a fairly smooth treatment experience, and recovery period (cancer free 9 years now). I attribute that completely to my family's support, the amazing medical team I had, the amazing community and natural abundance of the island, the career artist emergency grants I received from the Gottleib Foundation and the Haven Foundation, and my nature art as healing source. When life forced me to take this long pause, it nudged me to do more intense natural self discovery, if I was ever going to share with others what that truly means, and why more of us need to embark on this journey. I have firmly concluded that our lives, as individuals and a collective species, has a gaping hole without a deep connection to nature and art, and lour lives as "whole humans" now literally depends upon on us to stop ignoring them, minimizing them, dismissing them as "woo," and start taking these vital forms of intelligence seriously.

So here we are, after the past decade of more loss and grief, mixed with some incredibly beautiful moments, I present a version of Natural Self Discovery packed full of surprising new data, research and observations I have acquired from my recent graduate school studies. It also combines observations of the changes within myself and others during humanity's collective "forced pause" from the COVID-19 pandemic, along with the recent onslaught of natural disasters, divisions from identity politics and profound economic shifts.

Throughout this book, you will see feathers to indicate "pause" often, as an invitation to explore growth in moment-to-moment, situational events. "Forced pause" is the best way I could describe those life events and moments where life literally halts us in our tracks.

This book will remain in a the natural cyclical process of transformation, of Pause, Reflect, and Respond. Because that is our reality, a mirror to laws of biological life: the meaning of "life" is to sustain life through regenerative cycles, transformations triggered by external pressures. Yes, I have basically summed up our lives to that of a simple cell: yet that is the genius and reality of the design of nature, and all we are is an ecosystem of cells. Welcome to a process of "lightening up."

I hope you might allow this lifelong artist, entrepreneur, and nature-connecting guide, who can now be considered an expert on ambiguity tolerance, take you on a journey of discovery into increasing your ambiguity tolerance, creating a habit of immersion exploring your inner knowing of how nature thinks, and how your innate artist thinks. It is our dominant limited-linear binary thinking that has suppressed or severed this knowledge from us, yet it can, and must, be restored.

My hope is your journey here is the smoothest experience into a realistic and safe space to help move into awareness, acceptance, and initiative to try exploring and discovering what I call, "busting out of the binary and getting messy process." We were all taught to avoid "messy," and it is this story which causes us to feel the discomfort, and run in our fear of ambiguity. This book is for those who are ready to get messy, to get curious, and to investigate how our dominant human-centric thinking is holding us hostage, and learn the way out. This book is for anyone who does wish to learn how to get comfortable getting uncomfortable – ready to face an empty canvas full of possibilities, strategies and tools to help you navigate your way into a more harmonious life experience that is more accurately aligned with your natural unique talents and purpose. I aim to keep it simple and general reference most of the research, so this book is not another onslaught of the data and "shoulds"." We have all had enough of that. And it's this dynamic which has inevitably caused us to remain in a strange form of hopelessness, a shame-based story that creates a fearful, avoidant form of apathy. A gaping hole, a feeling that something is missing.

My aim is to introduce a way to help us disrupt those dominant stories and thinking processes which no longer serve us, and create a natural balance within ourselves where we have a calm confidence grounded in our naturally creative sensory intelligences and sensibilities. We can learn to glide with a calm confidence grounded in our unique values and purpose (aware of the stories imposed upon us that told us what our values and purpose "should" be), to keep us driven, engaged and excited about our life adventure.

You will discover that I am very much a balanced realist who can allow myself to vacillate between pragmatic analyzing and whole picture ideation. I have been balancing both fairly well so far, which helps me feel confident that I can share how I did with you.

A quick note on politics and religion: I consider myself a pedestrian on our shared planet, just as I consider all my fellow humans. We have all entered this planet as beautiful ecosystems, so we are all meant to be here, and we all have a right to discover, live and thrive in our unique natural creativity and sense of purpose. I remain in my truth from the natural and creative world of the ambiguous, where every situation can have multiple lenses, perspectives, and truths. Therefore, I refuse to ascribe to any entity that divides with controlling binary stories which perpetuate the extreme thinking that has created the mess we are now in. So, I will stay in my values and truth, while also able to listen to all views because we all have our own lens and experiences. It is by staying in curious exploration of all the possibilities, with many minds, many lenses, the willingness to get into the "messy" process of collaborating in our shared human experience on this planet together that we have a chance to experience harmony within ourselves, with each other and with our planet. We have a chance to work together towards our next stage of "homeostasis" within ourselves and the natural world, transform into our next phase of development, or, my favorite: travel together in our next frontier of maturity as a species.

You might have heard the phrase that it is about asking the right questions. So I must warn you, this journey together here will most likely present you with more questions than answers initially, yet I can promise you, if you pause long enough with nature as your primary support, and zoom out far enough, you will eventually have the confidence to move out of our collective human embedded shame story, to start connecting dots from your unique experiences and frame of reference to create a trail of your own understanding and strategic path toward solutions that work within your unique purpose on this planet. It worked for me, so that is why I am sharing this process with you.

I aim to do this in the most respectful and empathetic way, yet aware as a mere human in the natural bias, emotive condition, and limited bandwidth that science has shown comes with being human, I am fully aware that not everything I share will apply to all. I will do my best to indicate with a feather symbol when a sensitive subject or a word or phrase could possibly trigger an emotive reaction and assist in taking pause.

I accept that I will never be fully right from my limited lens in my identities and culture I was raised in. By learning to release my indoctrinated need to be right, I extend a heartful outreach and invitation to explore our differences while staying grounded in our primary shared interests' humans: survival, safety, security, health, belonging, self-esteem, and unique purpose on this planet. Even on a committed lifelong journey to expand my understanding and empathy for all lenses, cultures, and unique individual life experiences that myself, nor any one human can ever fully know your unique truth. All we can do is identify which experiences we share and have the willingness to connect with through the difficult conversations. The difficult conversations which we all know our human stories over the centuries has taught us to avoid.

In my unique identities as an American, generation X, white woman, Scottish-Irish-Austrian-Jewish descendant, child of divorce, latchkey kid, Catholic High School graduate, widowed mother of two, breast cancer survivor, member of multiple recovery groups and in CPTSD therapy, nature and art lover, painter, entrepreneur from a family of entrepreneurs, and lifelong learner with nature and art, I fully understand that my frame of reference is not yours. I enjoy the process of discovery and connection with all my fellow humans. As it is courageous curiosity and brave discussions which help us mature as a species and co-create solutions rather than perpetuating the problems.

So, thank you for spending your life moments here with me in this book. I mean this deeply, as I value life moments in my cost/benefit analyses at a very large sum, because there is no amount of money or stuff that can buy those back. I appreciate your quest for answers, your curiosity, and the honor of your time to at least explore some possibilities with me.

I fully understand now more than ever after my leadership journey, that our society still is struggling to grasp the importance of the non-verbal and sensory intelligence language of the natural world and the artistic process. My heart aches to help others restore these natural abilities that our modern societal thinking suppressed or took away, which is the core of why this book exists. I hope to create more materials, host natural creative experiences over the coming decades during my next phase on this planet, and look forward to those who connect and align with me to ensure we help restore these natural abilities, because every human has a right to thrive and experience life with these restored and fully intact.

In this space, for these moments we are together here as part of the human family - and my hope is we can pause just long enough to really sit in our collective reality as a species, now a very lonely, isolated species, that very much need kinship with each other and our fellow earth beings.

Sending you the warmest wishes that this book at the very least helps you make sense of the nonsense going on in our "non-sensory" modern human world, so you feel lighter in heart, mind and spirit. I hope you enjoy creating your unique relationship with nature as life force and exploding with creativity and drive aligned with your passionate purpose. I hope it helps you give yourself permission to pause, and explore your life experiences, even the muddiest of times., to discover where you have emerged like a lotus.

I hope you give yourself permission to immerse into a process like a butterfly, allowing that quiet, yet at times messy space to emerge with fresh new eyes and wings!

I know you can do this. We can do this. And I already love you just for picking up this book. Thank you!

Harmony for People and Planet, Love, Pam

"Monarch Transformation" *P.Hoke*

PHASE 1

PAUSE

The opportunity to give ourselves permission to stop long enough for a sensible, naturally intelligent, situational assessment

Sunrise with Kuka ~ P. Hoke

During Covid, I got to stay with a family friend on an off the grid island, and with Kuka, the wonder dog. To me, he reminds me how intelligent all natural beings are compared to how humans are behaving.

CHAPTER 1

Will the real misfit please stand up?

"I can't go back to yesterday because I was a different person then."

~ Alice of Alice in Wonderland by Lewis Carroll

Is it just me, or does it feel like we are arguing about where to place the furniture as we are riding on the Titanic? As a collective species, a human family, now with access to data and connection with each other literally at our fingertips, it really does not have to be this way. I believe we can, as now a self-imposed lonely species, separated from our life source and each other, can restore balance within an imbalanced mindset that has created some very real problems for us all.

Just as I have spent many years trying to be what others said I should be, I have recently discovered that modern society seems to have fallen into a similar trap. It seems we, as a collective modern society, have been sucked into a syndrome of sorts, a collective madness perhaps, where we have created an imbalance. We have become obsessed, addicted to our conveniences, modern comforts, status and stuff. It's like we are stuck in a story, a human-centric story that omits the very source that sustains our ability to live, the natural world, specifically our life source, Earth. From decades in this dominant, human-centric, limited binary thinking, our brains have successfully created a continuous loop that mirrors the addiction process. We now exist in a consumerism-based and shame-based culture where we tend to judge ourselves and others based on job titles or how much stuff we own and over-indulge in many things to fulfill. We seem to have forgotten about nurturing, our own health and well-being. It seems we lost our natural selves and trusting in who we naturally are, and then accepting others for who they naturally are.

This is not a "I know it all" telling you what to do book. Nor is it a gloom and doom data dump, or guilt trip. This is a book that discusses the facts and research of what is happening, who it affects. It points out the two realities of which no matter how much data, research and articles discuss them, our collective minds in how things still operate, have yet to fully validate and take real steps to address them. They are:

1. OUR NATURE DEFICIT DISORDER

As coined by Author Richard Louv

2. OUR CREATIVE DEFICIT DISORDER

I don't know if anyone has called it this so here I am calling it

Avoiding these two realities is what is ailing us, it is what has made "us" as humans, the misfit species as a whole, however, we individually have been muddling around in our own story that we misfit. Why?

The inconvenient truths of our insanity

The circumstances of late: increased mental illness, depression, violence, cancer, learning disabilities, obesity, hoarding, extinctions, cyber-wars, and climate crises. The abundance and availability of statistics and facts (thanks to our technology) demonstrate clearly a drastic mental shift in humanity is urgent if we are to survive. It has become quite clear that our chase for status and stuff, our desperate need to cling to our conveniences and comforts of modern living has not only made us sick, yet every day we see right before our eyes, how this has made the very source that allows life, earth, very sick. This dynamic, we all sense deep inside is insanity, yet we feel helpless in how to escape it, similar to an addiction. I recently heard author Seth Godin (now founder of the Carbon Almanac) called it our addiction to convenience.

We cannot live without earth, without nature...and once we realize we are very much nature ourselves, that we are not separate, we can begin to heal this vital relationship on the deepest, purest level, rather than superficially, or in a performative "check-off-the-boxes" - we can begin to truly walk our talk into the next phase of humanity. And although we have made great strides to address children's' awareness, what about the adults truly walking their talk? So, yes, this book is for the adults. It's time to mend our relationships with ourselves, our fellow adult humans, and our shared planet. We are the ones in the position to create the solutions that are so urgently needed. We are the ones who are responsible for showing our youth through actual shifts in our mindsets and sensible behaviors that are more aligned with our life source. There is no denying that Nature is now openly nudging us to do this, all we need to do is zoom out and look around. We are in a "forced pause" moment.

The research, the "experts," and the organizations and institutions all agree, our species is in trouble. And the evidence continues to show that most agree that it is more collaborative, adaptive, and conceptual skills grounded in increasing our emotional intelligence is what is necessary for our individuals and societies to survive and thrive as we enter the reality of our new economy and our new climate.

You might have heard the phrase that it is about asking the right questions. So I must warn you, this journey together here will most likely present you with more questions than answers initially, yet I can promise you, if you pause long enough with nature as your primary support, and zoom out far enough, you will eventually have the confidence to move out of our collective human embedded shame story, to start connecting dots from your unique experiences and frame of reference to create a trail of your own understanding and strategic path toward solutions that work within your unique purpose on this planet. It worked for me, so that is why I am sharing this process with you.

I aim to do this in the most respectful and empathetic way, yet aware as a mere human in the natural bias, emotive condition, and limited bandwidth that science has shown comes with being human, I am fully aware that not everything I share will apply to all. I will do my best to indicate with a feather symbol when a sensitive subject or a word or phrase could possibly trigger an emotive reaction and assist in taking pause.

I accept that I will never be fully right from my limited lens in my identities and culture I was raised in. By learning to release my indoctrinated need to be right, I extend a heartful outreach and invitation to explore our differences while staying grounded in our primary shared interests' humans: survival, safety, security, health, belonging, self-esteem, and unique purpose on this planet. Even on a committed lifelong journey to expand my understanding and empathy for all lenses, cultures, and unique individual life experiences that myself, nor any one human can ever fully know your unique truth. All we can do is identify which experiences we share and have the willingness to connect with through the difficult conversations. The difficult conversations which we all know our human stories over the centuries has taught us to avoid.

Let's be clear, Earth is purely being its natural, sensory intelligent, sensibly regenerative self. It's not personal, yet now requires us all as responsible members of the human family, citizens of planet Earth, to have a reckoning and association with our true relationship with our life source. If we are ever going to create a sustainable existence, we must restore our thinking that is fully aligned with the source that is necessary for our existence. The numbers show clearly that it is fiscally and ethically irresponsible to avoid this. A brief scan online of the abundance of spreadsheets shows clearly the costs of recent natural disasters and what it has already cost us by ignoring

decades of scientific evidence of what was happening. It is also irresponsible just in the primal sense, that primal NEED to live, and pause long enough to just grieve and fill the yearning that we all share to survive. Our avoidance is due to what Author Richard Louv brilliantly calls our Nature Deficit Disorder.
With the abundance of data, history, literature, podcasts, coaching, self-help, therapy and learning modules right at our fingertips, why is it that we still avoid allowing ourselves to include the perfection of nature's sensory, adaptive intelligence into our thinking process and language? Why is it that very few address the fact that due to its ambiguous, infinite, transformative, and wordlessness it' s too scary. Due to its reliance on the biological senses, it is too personal for us as a lonely species that now fears vulnerability (as Brene Brown has clearly proven). The uncertainty is frightening in our current limited human-centric binary thinking to learn this new language, and gosh forbid connect and feel with it.

The Universal Languages

Nature's language is a universal language of the sensory intelligence of life cycles, the universal language of communication of all species that is beyond words (as author Carl Safina). Then add in our natural abilities to make, create and ideate from our primal NEED to do so - our universal language expressed through the arts, music, design and all forms of unique expression and ideation. As author Daniel Pink has demonstrated clearly for decades, we are not using our "whole minds," at least in terms of our creative competencies, and our organizations are operating in outdated thinking processes which do not include our primal needs for autonomy, mastery, and purpose to thrive as human beings.

Amidst the urgent call to “care” about nature and others, we remain intellectually, physically, and emotionally disconnected from our shared life source and each other.

Amidst the urgent calls, the research showing we need to be both: more, adaptive, creative (conceptual skills) and care more about others (emotional intelligence - empathy), we have yet to begin to include and value the self-discovery process of who we naturally are, and fully using our innate creative and sensory intelligent competencies.

Why? Because they all are ambiguous. Each of these skills requires a willingness to embrace uncertainty. This doesn’t work for us in the way our modern minds have been groomed over the centuries. We have been trained to always “look” good, in control, don’t make mistakes, never be “wrong,” never color outside the lines, never get “messy” outside or with art supplies. If we do, shaming or “misfit” label ends up in there somewhere. Sound accurate?

This dominant, linear binary thinking, and an imbalanced reliance on data and the overanalyzing of our left brain, has shrunk our full capacities. We deem the creative process and nature connecting process, amidst all the proven direct benefits of both, as “woo,” or a waste of time, or not “productive.” Our insanity is staying locked in this thinking - which we are now attached to, because we have an outdated, embedded story that is now attached in our minds that tells us our status and stuff relies upon it. The reality is, staying attached to, addicted to this old story is what is now slowly killing our species, our spirit...a state of apathy when it comes to an authentic relationship with our life source.

We can realize our whole capacities, re-igniting our naturally creative and sensory intelligence, simply by restoring our nature-sense and art-sense. For decades now, author Richard Louv has called us out for not addressing our nature deficit disorder, and author Dan Pink has called us out for not using our whole minds in conceptual age we are in. Research is everywhere that proves we need a connection with nature. Simply read any of the books by Richard Louv, founder of Children and Nature Network, or look up the research of Green Schoolyards, Forest Therapy, Nature Prescriptions. I have listed several books in the appendix. There is also endless research and articles on how we need to have creative skills realized to use our "Whole Minds." And yes, Daniel Pink wrote the book "A Whole New Mind" back in 2008 that makes the clearest case for this.

We must learn how to recover and value both our natural sensory intelligences and our innate creative competencies if we are to survive and thrive, as individuals and as a species. It is our next frontier. And those who can step into this realm of expanded thinking processes are the ones who will thrive and feel fulfilled.

We have corporate retreats, or creative brainstorm sessions, void of any deep sensory connection or association with the natural world that holds the sustaining collaborative secrets and universal sensory language we crave, and with supplies and activities reduced to markers, crayons, and time/cost limitations that devalue, even infantalize the true collaborative, conceptual powers, and universal language of the creative process. We never incorporate the cost of not including these priceless forms of intelligence and communication which our research shows clearly are exactly the path towards reaching our shared goals. Our imbalanced reliance on technology has now led to the absence of the infinite value of the tactile, human-based sensory process that fully ignites our collaborative, cognitive and conceptual capacities.

Yet, we wonder why we remain in this vicious cycle of separation and division, and inability to pause and zoom out to visualize the whole picture outside our limited lenses, our inability to increase our ability to visualize and empathize with our fellow humans and their frame of reference? When we can't even move outside and investigate our limited human-centric thinking that remains attached to old long-embedded stories which no longer serve us, we will not be able to resolve our most pressing issues.

We are all works in progress! How do we learn without exploring, meandering? Just like trees that grow strong and branch out, weathering the winds, or paintings that emerge one paint stroke at a time. It is time for us to enjoy the journey of what we grow into, yet allow ourselves to accept ourselves, others, and the natural world around as pure, beautiful and all part of an ecosystem of intelligent love. Hopefully we have zoomed out here enough to acknowledge that it is not us as individuals who are the misfits, the imbalanced dominant thinking that is the misfit - making our species the misfit in a perfectly designed, intelligently regenerative natural system.

I have diligently journaled for years documenting my lived life experiences, testing my hypotheses, gathering research, articles, and observing events, shifts and movements over the last two decades. I also recently embarked on obtaining an expanded macro-lens and firmer grasp of how our current systems can shift within new adaptive leadership spaces in graduate school. Then took it even further with a certificate in Sustainability analysis. From this, I offer the two main activities which must now become valued, normalized and prioritized as if our lives depend on them, because they do. Experiences, processes and narratives which align with and include how nature thinks and operates, and incorporating the creative process as now essential adaptive elements for successful transition into our new conceptual economy and climate.

I will do my best to make the case for why we need to apply to our personal, familial and professional careers, yet also how they are applicable for groups, movements, teams, organizations, institutions, and governments to both accelerate and enhance our adaptation experience.

I first invite us into a "pause" phase to observe, and take a real situational assessment of what is happening with humanity, (Chapters 1 -4). My hope is you stick with me and dare to dig deeper as we move into a "reflection" phase (Chapters 5-8), where we learn to see ourselves as nature would, connect some dots, and ways to begin building our individual strategy around sensing and valuing our unique natural creative intelligences. Then, with hopefully some understanding, there is motivation to become one's natural self to gain the confidence in "becoming" such. I will share some tips that worked for me, and hope they might ignite your natural creativity so you can make your own trails and develop strategies that work best for you. I will do my best in this Respond phase (Chapter 9-12) to help you effectively plug in both the intelligence from natural world and creative world to expand your life experience, fulfillment and effectiveness in purpose. I created several trail maps to inspire and assist you on your journey.

We have two gaping holes in our modern thinking and systems: we are still operating within a limited linear, binary mindset, where we are not valuing immersion into the activities which continue to be proven to increase the adaptive, collaborative, cognitive and conceptual competencies that articles and research papers continuously state we need. Many are still nodding and saying yes, attempt surface "performative" activities to check off the boxes, yet in our fear of ambiguity, we still merely touch the surface, or avoid it completely. I recently heard a renowned expert on leadership talk about all these skills, with some brilliant ways to build them in teams, only to hear him end his talk with, "sometimes, however, I just end up with an art project." This tells me everything: it sums up the lack of understanding of the valuing the intelligence, collaboration, sensory experiential knowledge, and new connecting forms that "just an art project" reveals. It reveals that it is a language that, because it does not have quantifiable words or numbers, the information is completely missed.

Letting go of our "Misfit" Story

In a thinking system that is designed to keep us in a shame-based spiral so we do reach for the "more" we think we need, we have all accumulated a lot of stories about ourselves. Yet, these stories were implanted within us like a computer chip. We have a lot of software that has been downloaded which no longer serves us, in fact, most of it has a lot of bugs, and we could all could use an upgrade.

So many of us were punished when showing creativity when it didn't fit into the societal mold. To fill the voids or soothe these original hurts or feelings of being misfits, some of us had to either swallow it down with our bodies noting the shaming as danger. Some of us drown that natural creative spirit to "fit in" and make the world around them more tolerable. I believe we all suffer from some form of our modern societal indoctrination, these patterns that are now barriers holding us back from living the genuine, emotional, and physical lives were meant to live. No one can deny how much better they feel after being outdoors, we crave fresh air after being indoors too long whether we are consciously aware of it or not. It is time to stop devaluing the ultimate values of nature to our mental state of mind, beyond the obvious physical benefits – like keeping us alive. When did we start de-valuing our life source?

Our modern societal thinking keeps shoving this simple approach off the table, and because of that, we all hurt very deeply. We hurt because we are turning our backs on our life source. It is because nature is nameless, without the language we humans have created, so it is foreign to those of us who are living in modern societies, or even if we "know" we keep it to ourselves to avoid the discomfort of the shaming.

"Real" life, is right outside those walls, and we are only being cruel to ourselves and our children for denying ourselves our inborn rights.

I struggled in math and any subject that focused on linear thought patterns because I was a right-brain dominant, creative individual. I now know I have many super intelligences that go far beyond what our over-intellectual educational system and bump-and-grind corporate world could ever possibly comprehend or bottle up to capitalize upon.

And so do you. So does every human being and natural inhabitant on this earth. All living beings have inborn natural super intelligences that are completely unique, and yes, are of extremely high value to modern society. The big issue is that modern society forgot that this part of us and has led to a sort of amputation of our souls, our inner natural beings. We can re-learn how to plug in this missing ingredient that allows us to think with our whole minds. We can re-learn how to balance our brains naturally, creatively adapt, survive, and peacefully flow with changes of the incredible living organism we live on, earth.

If we merely zoom out and observe our behavior from the lens of that natural world, we perhaps appear just like an alcoholic who knowingly destroys their liver with every drink, or the smoker hurts their lungs, we continue to poison and destroy the very life-giving source we need to survive. We are like the line of ants blindly following each other to their eventual drowning – a sort of collective suicide if you really think about it. This is all just to avoid looking at the world as if our life source matters.

We only keep harming ourselves and our enjoyment of life by continuing to avoid and deny who we naturally are: organisms on a planet who can't pull ourselves out of what we now know is just a story. The story is so real in our minds that we have become so disconnected from and unaware of the real story - the "real" world that keeps us alive, the natural world.

I hurt for others suffering on both the surface and underneath hidden deep inside their souls in the society we've created. I feel that missing link is getting back to our emotional roots, deepening our connection with nature and our natural creativity, so we can begin to think clearly and sensibly again about what really matters first: breathing, eating, etc. – Remember, the basics?

We can balance this out after and find ways to harmonize our new ways by nurturing and respecting where we came from. As I ventured on this journey to discover some sanity amidst this increasing insanity, I began to discover that so many others were experiencing similar imbalances, just different flavors and levels of the craziness, depending on their identities and status in this dominant hierarchical thinking.

I relate to Jack Nicholson's character in the movie "As Good As It Gets," – "Don't sell crazy here, we're all stocked up." I feel it really is time for us as individuals to address our own personal imbalances, take responsibility for ourselves rather than continue to rely on waiting for the "specialists" to come up with solutions – as we have seen lately, they aren't doing such a fabulous job. We can take responsibility for ourselves and create the life experience we want, then share with others just by being who we are meant to be. We can heal that amputation from our inner nature and deep sensory aptitude and awareness and think with our whole minds again, so we can make sensible decisions rather than blindly following that self-destructive ant march.

I really feel fortunate to have the specific adversities and challenges I did throughout my life because guess what, I became accustomed to being a misfit, and accustomed to the challenges. Perhaps some of it we can say, helped us build resilience, yet it is also just as important to acknowledge which parts caused us harm so we can now remedy those harms by moving forward.

Anyone who has had first-hand experience with alcoholism or any other "-ism" can attest that only the one who has "been there done that" is the only one who can truly understand another's similar predicament. So perhaps we can together recover from our "mis-fit-ism?" We can re-write that now.

After years of zooming out, especially now understanding the truths of how it was a gradual hijacking of our natural thinking processes in alignment with the natural world and our natural human-beingness, I feel disgust, anger, and all the stuff. It does take a lot of journaling, walking, and communicating with nature, and a lot of messy unleashing with pencils and paints for me.

I find myself very grateful for the strengths from the adversities of living as a creative in a non-creative world provided as an artist and self-employed designer. It helped build this resilience were the realities of dealing with rejections, within the competitiveness of creative fields. Yet, as we have all experienced, most jobs and industries operate in this competitive mindset, even communities do now from our current dominant societal thinking. Yet, this competitive mindset is what rules over collaborative, and we now know, it no longer serves us, or our right to a sustainable and thriving life on this planet.

This competitive mindset we can see has resulted in the fear of "failure" which leads to that fear of being shamed or labeled as a "misfit.

My question to you is this, as I ask myself this often, as more and more reveals itself: How were you conditioned from the beginning by society to feel like a misfit?

Do you tend to have that inner sense that you are not doing enough, not doing things "right," or doing it "wrong?"

Well, if the answers are yes, it is normal, we are all born perfectly, uniquely human, yet along the way society's civilized "advancements" and "progress," we tipped over the edge into a sort of make-believe, unobtainable false image of perfection. We pay lip service to being ourselves, while every moment we are somehow "fed" that we need to be more or are still not good enough. We forget to acknowledge our health and survival truly lies in self-care – not selfishness as society and our family structures have labeled it.

Self-care is critical, because if we do not care for ourselves, we do are not loving ourselves. So, how can we possibly really care for or love anyone or anything else? This is balance we can learn from our life source in nature, because nature is a perfectly balanced system, helping us learn to balance self-care with empathy and responsibilities. By studying and spending time observing nature, we can learn to make sense of what is our responsibility and what is not. Nature also helps us validate our unique intelligences, instincts, and inherent creative abilities, to trust ourselves, and let go of the doings and saying of others. We can get on with our lives and still be loving individuals – just individuals with renewed self-respect.

So now we can shift the narrative: the misfits are the ones who continue to perpetuate this dysfunctional, dominant human-centric binary thinking that continues to hinder actual "growth" of the natural human mind?

So, will the real misfits please stand up? If I know anything now, as I see with my own eyes and sense in my soul what is happening in the world, that it is becoming more and more obvious that the real misfits are the ones who refuse to see how the only true freedom and chance for survival of humans, is for us to free ourselves to be naturally, perfectly human – just as nature intended. Yet, we must ask ourselves, if we are keeping in that story that dismisses our natural creative competencies and connection with our life source, nature, then aren't we still in the misfit story? We are if we aren't taking steps towards within ourselves to restore our natural minds, our natural creativity that considers the natural world as our kin.

We have become so numb, many of us we are no longer even consciously aware of what's missing. I want to help introduce a way to help fill that something missing and hope perhaps this approach will penetrate and prick on that numbness just a little, because I can attest, once that feeling is back, there is no stopping the flood of good vibes that comes with it! Imagine if we all began to discover our own inner peace with nature how that would affect how we treat ourselves, others, and our planet. At least we could know we tried and did what we could to enjoy our time living in peace and fully, consciously connected to the incredible living organism that gives us life, earth. We get to give ourselves permission to leave the misfit story as the current dominant system of human thinking is "misfit" because it is insanely halting the evolutions and the survival of our species at this point.

So, it's this mis-aligned, misfit thinking that devalues our whole humanness, and the value of nature and art. We have a right to a relationship with both, with all the expanded capacities and skills they offer. Let's reclaim them.

Ok, now that you have had to roll through these realities, I hope you might decide to dig further. Being courageously curious is living a fulfilling creative life, and one that is aligned with the "real" world, which, we now know is not our human-made story world. Our responsibility, to ourselves, is to free ourselves from the outdated, and irresponsible stories that are simultaneously destroying our habitat, our minds, hearts, and overall the spirit of humanity.

Here are some trail maps to help you begin to get a sense of this limited mindset which suppressed all of our other capacities, which we need to survive collaboratively, and strategically. We begin with simply jotting down what weighs heavy on your mind and heart with the Mind-Heart Trail Map (a larger version is in the tools section of this book, or downloadable PDF's are available on my website pamelahoke.com).

Now onto getting real with our place on this planet, leveling with the caterpillar.

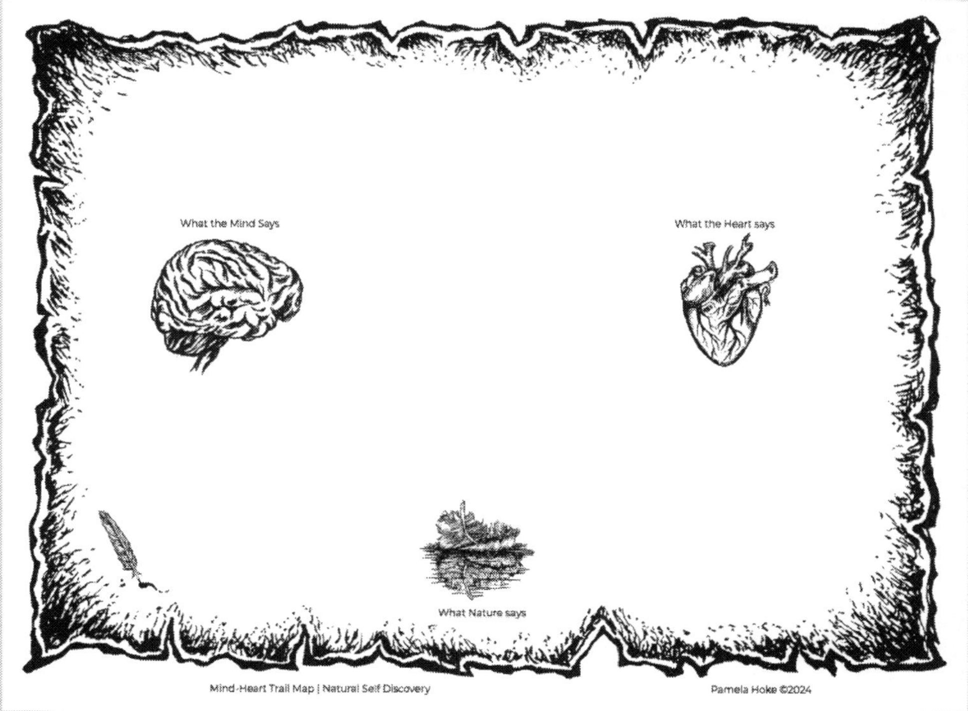

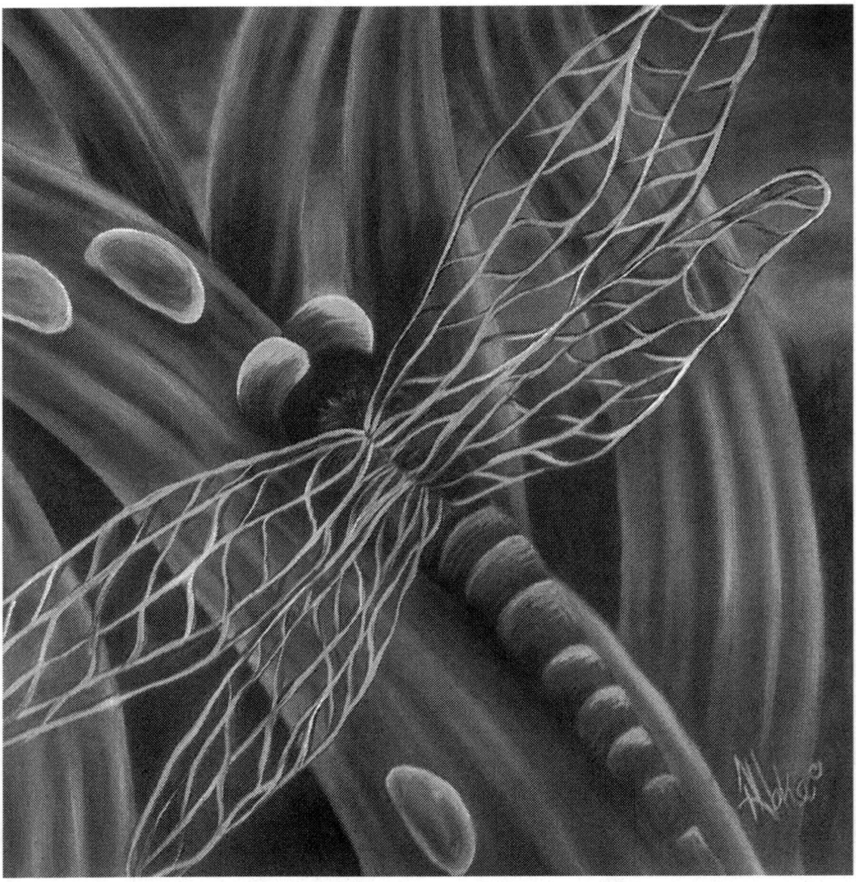

Golden Wing ~ P. Hoke

Dragonflies have a larval stage, just like Caterpillars, and both show me the perfect design and intelligence of natural life cycles. They teach me to respect, identify with, and relate to what they go through in their transformation process, They inspire me to embrace change, because if they can go through the messy part of transformation, so can I.

CHAPTER 2

Time to Level with the Caterpillar

"Who are You?" asks the Caterpillar
"Who are Your?" asks Alice
"Who in the world am I? Ah, that's the great puzzle."
The Caterpillar ~ Lewis Carrol, Alice in Wonderland

Now that we have covered who the real misfit is according to the realities of the natural world, our life source, let's get into some more reality of our place in the Universe. This helps us get to better be able to take in some real truths of our situation during our pause phase together.

Who are we?

Many may experienced a neat visual exercise in kindergarten, where you lay on a huge sheet of paper, someone traces your body silhouette, then the teacher asks you what is special about you, and begins to write those words inside your body outline. You are then asked to color it. This is actually a great start to do now as an adult or emerging adult. We have to begin somewhere – and this is the somewhere. Even a simple outline, yet then take it further, your body with nature around it, and then other humans. Usually it is easier to just put ourselves in nature, as due to our now growing resentment of our current dominant destructive thinking, many of us have an underlying resentment of other humans. Those who have been most oppressed by our dominant systemic thinking have every right to be, and I challenge us all, to explore that resentment as the possible reason as to why research shows we prefer connecting online over in-person whenever possible? Could it be this is why we are more connected than ever, yet research is showing we are the loneliest we've ever been?

Who are we from Nature's lens?

The best way for us to move forward in life is make that leap in really getting to know who we really are...and I do not mean the pre-determined mold or society conditioned us to become. If it's at all possible, please find a natural area or go near a natural being while you read this chapter, it may increase how you begin to answer this question, while also having support in processing the hard questions and truths we will be exploring.

We know from emotional support animal research, and nature connecting research, that natural beings energize us, provide us comfort, soothe anxiety, and help us escape and better navigate life as natural human beings in a world currently dominated by limited, linear binary thinking systems that have reduced us to human "doings."

As we truly begin this journey of restoring our relationship with nature, reconnecting with the natural world as kin, we need to begin to create a more fair and balanced relational view of nature and natural beings as reliable comfort to us. They are here to participate in life in harmony with us, and we will begin to experience this as love through this new expanded sense of belonging and support. This is the beauty of restoring our kinship. They delight us, they soothe us, they and their existence and role in ecosystems is what keeps us all alive. However, when we get into viewing who we are from nature's lens, we cannot deny that even in our "adoration" of these beings, in restored kinship, we still may continue to see them as our entertainment, our property, entitled to our right to access them often without their consent. If this feels eerily familiar, it is most likely you have experienced this from the oppression that is a result of the embedded mindset modern humanity currently is in.

Now, we could argue that we are the dominant species, as our dominant human-centric linear thinking stories have told us. Perhaps it's time we now begin to shift that thinking from a narrative of a superiority, domination, stewarding-over our kin, into a more collaborative, empathetic, grateful, respectful balanced relationship?

The "who are you" puzzle has been philosophized, and in my opinion, over-philosophized and analyzed for decades. Yet, done so from this dominant sense of superiority and dominion.

What we humans know for sure, is that knowing what and who we are is one thing, yet loving what and who we within the whole picture of natural life systems is another.

The question goes deep, and the next chapter take us even deeper. I will do my best to indicate when we enter a rather heavy subject with a feather such as above, to encourage the "pause" process which allows for the full mind and body check. It is best if this is combined with taking deep breaths to ensure mental space and energy to zoom out and visualize how the trails connect to an infinite amount of possible perspectives, lenses and circumstances. The whole picture lens can overwhelm our proven limited bandwidth, yet is truly the only way we can start learning how to bust out of the binary thinking we as humans can lock ourselves into. This is where I have found jotting things down and mapping out thought trails is so helpful, and relieving to the mind.

It is simply a biological feature of how our brains to loop into familiar thinking patterns, however, this is the opportunity to challenge ourselves to find comfort within the uncomfortable in-betweens. Assuring our brains we want to "go there," so we can intercept, or hack the loop. And it is safe, since we are not living in the Paleo days where we literally had to be in constant fight or flight mode, we now are free to learn strategic responsive techniques rather than living in that reactive cycle. Our systems as they are would prefer we stay in the impulsive, reactive, however, we can see clearly how that is no longer serving us. We only have to refer to the constant flow of articles and books addressing our physical and mental health issues, our relationship issues. and growing self-care industry.

What separates us from other species?

The most clear, and recent article on the answer to this question is from Scientific American, by Thomas Suddendorf. There are only two mental abilities that separate humans from animals, as research is finding more and more that there are many animals that match many of our cognitive skills. The two profound dimensions which set us apart are the ability "... to form nested scenarios, an inner theatre of the mind that allow us to envision and mentally manipulate many possible situations and anticipate different outcomes. The second is our drive to exchange our thoughts with others. Taken together, the emergence of these two characteristics transformed the human mind and set us on a world-changing path."

So, it is quite clear this is how we now are collectively looping in a dominant, linear, binary thinking process (one which dismisses the wordless sensory languages and intelligences of the natural and creative process worlds), and it is destroying us. This is truly going to take one massive mind hack. Yet I believe that with the narrative which effectively addresses the benefits to us directly, our loved ones, and our communities as a whole, it can be done. The brand marketer in me is completely convinced at this juncture, it is our job now to stop perpetuating the apathy with doom, and shift the narrative in a way that any marketer knows: sell "what is in it for me?"

"Whole" Humans

Here we are, at no fault of our own, not using all our human capabilities. My wish is to move us deeper into this – where we become "whole humans," and using our full mental and physical sensory intelligences. The limited binary thinking we are stuck in has led to still looping through an outdated chart, Maslow's Hierarchy of Needs. This is a prime example of what we will be exploring throughout this book of the need to adapt old research to what we know now. Regarding this chart, limiting our humanness to a stacked triangle in "order." The concepts, to credit Maslow, yes, are true. This is the part of the research that still works. What doesn't work is the limited "hierarchy" and stacked approach.

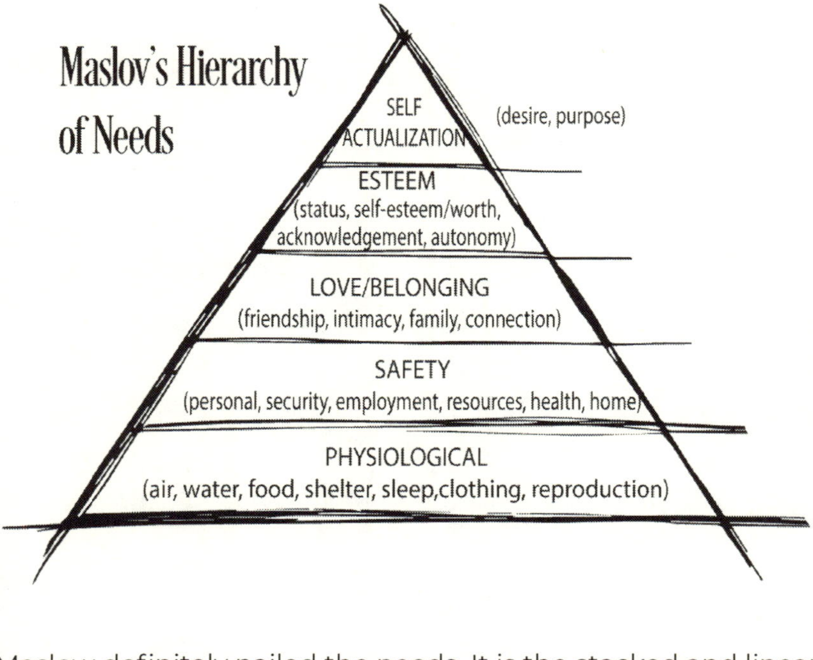

Maslow definitely nailed the needs. It is the stacked and linear part that does not work. Recent evidence, such as Covid's deaths of despair, shows clearly that human needs are circular, not stacked.

Here is my adaptation. I call it the "circle of human needs." It feels like a more adaptive, realistic model that accurately represents our true natural cycles

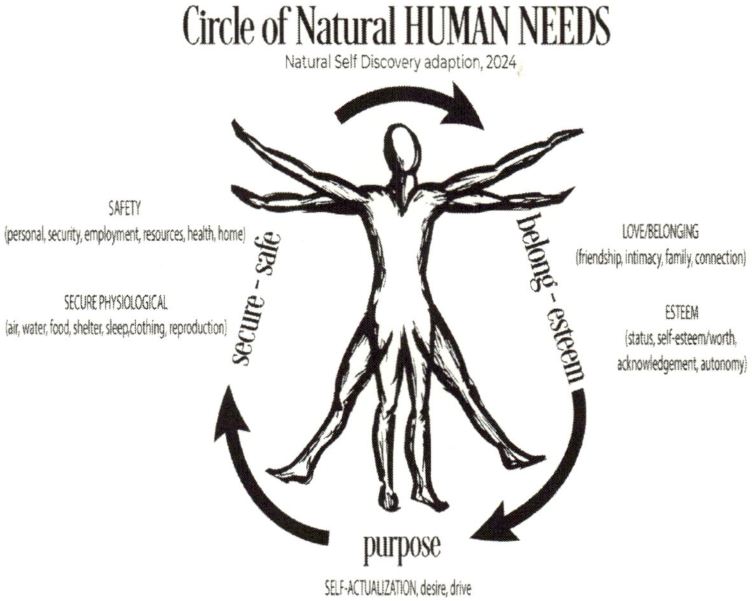

We definitely needed to ditch the word "hierarchy" simply to be more respectful to ourselves as living beings with similar needs, yet can vary related to our unique life experiences.

This is the language that perpetuates our limited thinking because just the word "hierarchy," not only suggests that binary, dominating mindset that has harmed us, it limits our uniqueness as a human who has a unique fingerprint. Every one of us has a unique fingerprint, so yes, we also have a unique formation of cells, unique experiences and cultural understandings, unique identities and frames of reference from our conditioning during our formative years. The word also keeps us in that "who we are" is dictated by someone else's story, and it's no mystery, as those of us who have experienced our teens years, this is where our early retaliatory behaviors manifested from. Our human need for autonomy and independence will always prevail no matter how much we try to stay in a dictated, societal "norm" story just to fit in. More of that "misfit" nonsense!

The Gift of "Pause"

Pausing to explore challenging topics such as these is necessary if we genuinely desire to feel some relief from the chaotic mindset we all have been living in. We can adapt and evolve by simply the openness and willingness to gradually become more courageously curious, to lean into the uncomfortable sea of ambiguity and unknowns. And there is no better place than to do this with our reliable, intelligent expert on adaptation and evolving: **nature**.

Creating a habit to pause and check ourselves in relation to the nature world sets a sense of belonging, and safety because the natural world wants you here (you're breathing with it and gravity keeps you attached), and it is the most reliable of any one thing or person we could ever imagine. Think about it. The air is delivering us oxygen each day, the oceans circulate to create the flow of it just for starters. I hope this becomes your prompt to revisit all the science studies from a new lens. Sadly, the studies were boring and dry to many, because they were void of any emotive attachment to life as a loving force that keeps us alive. It is rarely presented this way which has kept us feeling separate from it.

Connecting with the natural world can be a private, personal journey that goes on between just you and nature with no one else to interfere or judge. Unless, of course, you choose to keep judging yourself. Yet, I found the more I did it, I could not contain my deep sensory connection, which is now why you are reading this book, why my brand business is all about branding a relationship with nature as fashionable, and why my life of artwork is all centered in deep loving portraits of my connected feelings from my direct experiences with the natural world.

This is where thinking like, and in sync with natural systems comes to our rescue. To accept the fact that humans are storytellers and our species has created a whole heck of a lot of stories which are now in our minds, and secondly, we get to make safe space for ourselves to unpack said stories and discern which truly align with who we are in this moment and whether the story is serving us. This begins with that long overdue courageously curious list.

These human-centric stories are killing us

Remaining in this loop of dominant thinking is in direct conflict with our life source, the natural world is allowing us to rationalize and justify our addition to convenience, comfort, status and stuff. Our old embedded, dominant stories that center humans is not only becoming evident from the documented decline of our overall mental health and satisfaction with life, yet also our physical health, per the latest statistics from the World Health Organization. We are witnessing in live time our human health, safety from natural disasters, economic security, and attitudes decline in direct proportion with the health of our natural ecosystems, scarcity of the natural resources we need to survive. These old stories can be easily intercepted with new trails to ways of thinking that include the language and intelligence of our life source, so we not only benefit from the physical and psychological improvements by being more connected to it, yet we actually increase our natural cognitive, collaborative, conceptual and adaptive skill-sets to improve our safety, security and societal conditions. Let's face it, we have a human superiority complex.

Mapping it out

Creating a hand drawn map of stories, a trail that shows us before our eyes how they intersect, break, and impact ourselves and others helps our brain do its sorting, yet creates more bandwidth and capacity to process in our whole minds through this tactile sensory process and visual language. Also, using a tree outline helps because it can be a visual way of tracing the root thoughts, how they travel through us and branch out.

This concept for a story map, and all the maps created here, start with you – no one else . It is the invitation to explore visually, and fully sense and visualize the "whole picture" of your "whole humanness." The maps I've created are to inspire you to create your own, they are not meant to be a standard way of thinking (I think we all are sick of rigid standards). S the mapping process has to start with just you not thinking of anyone else except your relationship with yourself, period. Think of it as a personal story of yourself to help serve as a reference guide. From there, plugging in the natural world, and those who share similarities to your story, including beings in nature. Create metaphors, connections with both nature and others to help begin that sense of understanding, connecting the dots of the chain of thoughts, stories and how they impact you, the natural world as your life source, and your fellow humans around you.

The climate crisis is in our heads

It really is...literally and figuratively.

The climate crisis is an actual event, and does require us to process it. That is why there is now a movement of "Climate Conversation," Climate Talk, Climate Coffee, etc. There are even cards and activities designed simple to help us start the conversation around the changing climate. Preparing for the changes that will affect our safety, security and overall ability to adapt and survive is sensible, reasonable, rational, and intelligent.

It is important to note however, that it is how our heads process it, what story we weave in our minds around it. Like any traumatic or stressful event, our bodies will react with physical changes, and psychologists continue to point out that it is all about how we respond to these events. We cannot control our bodily reactions, yet we can control our though processes around it. So yes, we must move into processing how we are individually responding the climate changes, which, I remind you, is simply Earth being the incredibly, intelligent, regenerative organism it is, doing what it has done for thousands of years.

Whatever we resist, persists.

If we continue to tell our brains to ignore the underlying physical reactions, which is our intelligent senses knowing what is happening, the loop will continue until we address it. Unfortunately, as with any part of our sensory signals from life experiences, when we refuse to process them, physics tells us that signal energy has to go somewhere. So, with regard to the issue of climate change, our bodies know it is happening. A flock of birds sense when a storm is coming and responds with the appropriate action for them after assessing their options, which usually means to move away from the danger if conditions allow and is sensible, or take cover. For us as humans, if we continue to put off the conversations with ourselves and connect with others about it, our body will continually have those energy stress signals and send to our brains in a continual loop until we address it.

Now, depending on our decision to pause and process it - just face it and do a situational assessment, take the time to gather all information possible from many sources (as unbiased as possible), and compare to our individual situation, create a trail of options after listing or mapping our capacity and support. Once we actually stop resisting creating a strategy, the loop will stop because we have answered the signal from our natural senses. Our brain is then satisfied, therefore so is our body. This can actually create a sense of calm, a sense of confidence while still remaining in a sensible healthy form of awareness, rather than keeping in a "crisis" story to the point that it hinders our ability to strategize appropriate responses.

The old stories trap us in "group think"

Now, part of why I also state the climate crisis is in our heads is because we cannot ignore that it is the dominant binary-limited thinking which caused the current climate situation due to our imbalanced relationship with our planet. We can, from this dominant thinking unconsciously move into "group think," where our brain is trained to rationalize ways to protect the thinking that has provided us comfort.

Most of us know that the climate is no longer up for debate, yet in the case of a dear reader still questioning this, I kindly urge you to challenge whether or not your might be trapped in "group think." As we expand beyond our limited human-centric narrative that is omits the natural world, we receive relief from a habitual mind loop that is creating our inner chaos, which ripples outward. A start in this might be checking out how every single prediction in the a book from 2008,

The Inconvenient Truth" (whether you like Al Gore or not, he was right about what was going to happen)along with many others, including the profound Exxon Memo from an Exxon Oil researcher from 40 years ago, The US Climate Reports over the years, and endless studies by the Oil and Gas industry. Oh, and then there is the plastic Industry's trail of evidence of their climate impact, which led them to "invent" recycling just to halt alternative sustainable solutions and protect the demand for plastics. Then there is The Carbon Almanac, developed by marketing guru, and Author of Purple Cow, Seth Godin.

There are so many other deep reflections and research on our psychological and physical responses to what we are calling the "climate crisis, however, I wish to keeps us on track through our leveling with the caterpillar. And yes,, climate grief and anxiety is a real thing - all we have to do is take a few moments to search the endless documented shared traumatic experiences from victims of fire, hurricanes, snowstorms, floods, droughts and tornadoes.

Don't expect to fully know the answers, because the answers, if you are a natural human being, will change and adapt just as our climate does. That is the way it should be, for what would life be without the excitement of shifts, challenges and change?

"Life is either a daring adventure or nothing." ~ Helen Keller

The point here is to at least begin to think about who we are, and who we really want to be – NOT what others have told us or are still telling us to be. This only works if you take a genuine inventory, one taken in the purest form and in the purest environment. A personal inventory without the intellectual filters of what society and others tell us, but how we really feel. This can be done very effectively in nature, because nature only sends you cues...it doesn't judge you or dictate to you. The goal is to engage those sensory brain cells, get them fired up again to help you on a path to whole-mindedness, to use all of your brain without second-guessing it. This is trickier than it seems, because we have spent our entire lives in a habitual brain pattern of immediately second guessing ourselves, incorporating others in all our feelings and actions, and devaluing and invalidating our inner thoughts and feelings. With today's harried, indoor, and artificial object obsessed society, how can we possibly know our natural selves unless we are somewhere natural and pure? So back to the first recommendation, you may want to go outside if possible, sit in the bathtub in water, or sit next a pet or plant.

What are the first words or sentence that comes to your mind right away when asked "Who are you?"

Did you answer as if you were arriving at a party and someone comes up and asks the question in the sense that you were merely required to state your name and perhaps who at the party you were connected to? Or, did you dive right into the real meaning of the question and began pondering on the deeper meaning of the question? Could you dare to see yourself, and answer honestly how you see yourself genuinely, not you which you reveal to society and friends to fit in? Could you go further and detail how you see yourself and your role in the natural world.

Now...try this:

Who are you really...without your status or your stuff?

This is the part where we get to the real core of who one is, isn't it? Perhaps looking at is as the who we are wishing to be helps begin where our natural selves are – but first, we have to let go of our vice grip on what society and others tells us to be. Make a list, or create a trail map of "you" with only nature, your natural skills and what you like to do.

3 Questions we can ask ourselves.

My first recovery guide after embarking on the adventure of navigating life without relying on alcohol as my relief ten years ago shared these questions, which rocked my world. I ask myself these three questions at a minimum every week.

Are you doing what you want to do?

Are you living where you want to be living ?

Are you living with who you want to live with?

If you don't know, perhaps it is a good time to sit quietly with nature, outdoors or simply close to a natural being, and find out.

John C. Parkin, in his innovative book F**k It, presents an incredible concept in "curing" anyone of whining or complaining about their lives, but more importantly creatively places into perspective a quick way to help begin the process of you answering this question. Who Are You, without your status (job, etc.) and your stuff? A quick note: the occasional swear word will be used in this book. Why? Because they are just words, labels that in nature really do not matter, and honestly, it is quite the tragedy, and part of the severity of our societal illness of late. I read a great anonymous quote on Facebook: "It is sad that people are now more offended by a swear word than they are about global hunger, deforestation and illnesses." So, sorry, if you can't get over that, you may be would up tighter and more rigidly removed than you were aware. May I kindly suggest that you chill out for a while and be open to the notion that swear words are just words that we humans made up, and have attached too much meaning to them? Parkin boldly presents his book with this title as his creative way of saying to the world, that yes, we all need to chill out!

Here's The F**k It Therapy process in a nutshell, which may help you begin your "Who Are You without your status and stuff?" question: You are whining about your life, you feel upset or dissatisfied. It goes something like this, yet his version is much more hilarious: You hire the F**k It Team to cure you of your consistent unsatisfied with life feeling. The team seizes all your bank accounts, has your car repossessed, calls your boss with a nasty story to get you fired, your family leaves you, your mortgage company evicts you from your home. You are sitting out on the street all alone, with the clothes on your back wearing your watch, when the last of the F**k It therapy Team runs by and takes your watch, too. About 70-plus percent are cured. The point Parkin makes, and what I am trying to make here, is we do attach too much meaning to things. He also goes further to demonstrate we also attach to much meaning to people and happenings.

I like Parkin's book because the title completely suits the mission of the book, saying "f**k it" is therapy in itself. And, honestly, I can look to just about any of the wildlife around me, it is very clear from their reactions to us humans lately, they completely have that "f**k it" look – or perhaps, a "f**k you" look in their eyes. I can completely understand why much of wildlife has this attitude regarding humans these days. They are connected to the web of life more than we, and see us looking utterly ridiculous, if not completely childishly irresponsible in the way we have "unplugged" from the system. We are the outsiders now. But to, me, this also is that defining moment of character in us all, and essentially goes back to my stance on the core of our increasingly obvious "collective illness" in our "New Brain" society that has tipped off balance. This story may also seem eerily similar to those who have suffered from addictions that pretty much always end up coming to a screeching reality halt similar to this, well, if they are lucky that is. So many, more and more today, are not surviving their "bottoms."

Now, onto the next phase of this question:

"Who are you in nature's eyes?"

That is, how do you think nature sees you?

I am serious, here. Have you ever really considered what that bird who visits you really thinks? Or, you pets for that matter? Did you ever think about how a tree, a forest, or a plant feels when you are around them? Now our modern dominant "group think" tells us that would be weird, or not normal. However, Indigenous People would consider the opposite, the inability to be able to resonate, relate, and communicate with natural beings would be considered not normal.

"There's nothing wrong with having a tree as a friend."

\- Bob Ross

To really discover yourself, and feel good about yourself at the same time, Nature is your best teacher. How do you think nature sees you? Start by contemplating on the biological part of how nature sees your role of the whole the web of life. By going outside and just noticing the first signs of nature around you, a bird, a squirrel, a bug, or even a tree, and just sit quietly with it. The bird sees your face, your strange featherless body, your eyes. Any being in nature sees you just as you physically, biologically are – and nature also senses you be the vibes you send out, and, yes, acts accordingly.

The reason I bring up this question is to really help you start looking at nature in a more mutually consensual approach, a more respectful approach. Nature, essentially, does respect you, and does not seek out to harm you. Well, unless you are not in tune with nature, or sending out negative energy. When you are not in tune with your natural surroundings like our fellow inhabitants (the bees, birds, bugs and squirrels), your natural senses (or what we tend to call common senses), you can find danger. When you are aware, like a dog or bee that can sense fear, or sense when you are in harm's way, you are not in danger. This is the main point in beginning a deeper connection with nature – respect through being aware – awake to your surroundings! We have become number and less aware not only of natural surroundings, but even in traffic. Think about it. Most accidents happen because one or two people are not aware of what is going on around them. My theory is, if everyone was simply more tuned into their surroundings from a survival in nature mindset, our traffic accidents would decrease significantly.

Nature sees us either a part of, or disconnected from it, and does send signals. These signals can be extremely positive, such as an animal that senses you are respectful of it and mean it now harm will allow you to come closer. However, if you tromp through a flower bed with bees just trying to do their job, not in tune with their buzzing about enough to walk around their way, they will sting you. If you are in a predator's food territory, say swimming with a lot of little fish (there are generally big fish below wherever there are little fish, ask any surfer), or too close to a mother bear's cub, nature sees you as a threat. However, if you are fully in tune...aware...connected and feeling nature, your brain and awareness capacity heightens, and nature responds respectfully, because you innately feel respectful from the good feelings of just being aware. It's all about awareness, of self through what is around you – which will help you then begin to answer the question of who you are according to nature.

Why care what nature thinks of me?

Well, let's go back to basics here...we are nature because our biological make-up completely relies on it as a symbiotic system (just breathe or drink some water) – actually, we need nature more than nature needs us. Nature wants us here obviously, because here we are. What is has gone completely out of whack is we humans have placed ourselves into a collective illusion that we are somehow outside of nature, above it – when in actuality, it is our life source. Face it, we are permitted to be here as inhabitants of the full organism of earth – the sooner we get back to this core realization, we can begin to sense the unconditional love that we receive every moment we take in air or drink water. Once we begin feeling a deeper sense of this on an emotional level, we can then start the incredibly journey to discovering our role in participating in this web of life, (and enjoy it) yet with heightened senses and awareness – fully awake with all brain cells firing. We can finally rise beyond just our human invented language-based intellectualism we have become so addicted to, and begin to balance both. Care what nature thinks because nature loves you unconditionally – what do you do when someone loves us? Do we love them back, or at least appreciate it and say thanks?

This question begins our journey of a more respectful approach to nature, that helps us to tap into an ancient wisdom and creative ingenuity that has been there all along. It helps us connect new brain cells that have been numbed out because our human-made language system and intellectual puffery has snuffed them out. Becoming more aware of and fully acknowledging our presence with nature, not just beside it, but breathing with it and actually thinking with it, awakens a long lost love inside and pulls up new intelligences and insights, new feelings. Many shy away from this brave step because of the initial discomfort of feelings, just like when your leg or arm falls asleep from sitting in a strange position – as it awakens, those strange tingles begin. We know to ride through them because eventually the leg or arm will soon regulate and feel comfortable.

Biologists, chemists and environmental scientists all acknowledge nature teaches us, yet, we just keep forgetting to fully give it credit for doing so. Why? Because the information obtained gets taken to be used to hurt nature, therefore it is quite obvious that the sensory part of a full connection with nature is gone. We have to call feeling simple vibes from nature fancy, nature disconnected labels such as "inter-species communication," which creates sensing and feeling nature's non-language signals as some sort of voodoo. Oh, please. Can we just cut out this over-intellectualizing and just acknowledge sensory vibrations, the actual brain waves and signals that physics fully acknowledges as intelligence exchanges? It is getting utterly ridiculous that we have to continue to disconnect from the reality these signals, or any of our instincts really are

– these are our very own truth as we know it. No one can take them away, ever, as long as we are breathing participants in earth's system. They are very much natural intelligences – our intelligence. Nature is one large system with molecules, and yes we are molecules, communicating with each other. I don't have to write some long boring scientific paper to prove this, because we all feel it in our gut and know it through pure feeling. Why do we no longer allow ourselves to trust in it as we did pre-civilization? Imagine being able to balance this with living in today's world. It is completely possible...we just haven't given ourselves permission to validate it as real even though it is right before us. We are hooked into this mantra that the "real world" is the made up world of humans. After the beautiful camping adventure, or peaceful walk in the park, many will say, "oh, back to the real world, now." Really? What is the real world, I ask. I see a tree, and I see reality. I sense my thirst for water, and that is a biological reality. Are we really that brainwashed? Hmmm... just something I dare you to ponder on with regard to what is real and what is not, as this may assist in you really getting to know the natural you, but more importantly, acknowledging and trusting that the natural you is very much real and not some fantasy. You are not crazy –in fact, in my opinion, everyone else is if they are out of touch with their natural selves.

I sometimes sense wildlife looking at us humans as not only extremely rude, yet stupid because we continue to avoid emotionally plugging in to fully sense their non-verbal communications as a very valid form of language – as if ours so superior. We are so removed from the whole gig...and they see the obvious. I think most of nature is laughing at us as we carry about so busily in ludicrous inefficiency when it comes to true survival tactics. I actually believe nature now may be laughing at us, but also crying inside at the same time – mostly out of feeling sorry for us because we are missing out on the real sensory communication party of life. And sadly, the reality is, Earth will just keep going with or without us. It's not personal, it's just the restorative, regenerative, sensory genius of the natural world - life sustaining life.

I know many biologist friends who had to leave corporate positions due to their inner nature, their capacity to feel with and sense nature's communication. This pull was stronger, and they sensed that inner conflict of using nature, and the conflicting story of staying emotionally separate from it.
We are welcome here, yet just like what we would expect from a house guest, nature does want us to enjoy its resources...yet respectfully and sensibly, so the system can sustain itself. It is no longer a "woo" tree-hugger statement to care for and love our life source, to create an authentic symbiotic relationship, as it is now our key to survival.

We need nature more than nature needs us. We also need creativity and the arts to expand our capacity to connect with and discover ways to live in alignment with nature.

Research continues to show that contact with nature increases our endorphins, creative,adaptive, cognitive and collaborative competencies, mental and physical health all while decreasing stress levels (cortisol), disease, and disorders. And what most climate and nature therapy experts forget to connect, is that connection with the growing research of how the creative process and engagement with the arts in all forms produces the exact same benefits! Just like creativity experts can level up by incorporating the natural world into their frameworks, climate and science experts can level up by incorporating the creative world into their frameworks.

This not only accelerates our shared interest in simple survival, yet to thrive as "whole humans." It goes far beyond the lip service of taking a walk in the park, or doing a paint and sip night – we need to expand beyond talking the talk, and checking off our "performative" boxes, yet really, fully immersing...walking our walk. The research and data is all out there, and we now have a combination of two incredible solutions.

Placing "Who are you" into perspective naturally, and watch how relationships with others can improve

Nature sees us through a lens of a biological, mutually consensual symbiotic relationship. This is we as human organisms do for the most part – what we have set out of whack is the "mutual" part. I have found myself guilty of this often. "Who are you" question is mostly to begin a new lens of knowing, trusting, understanding, and appreciating your place in nature. It is not to shove yourself into other's business and responsibilities that are not yours.

Observe with good vibes, yes, but not try to change or alter the course unless there is an obvious calling, permission, from that being to do so. (My, if we only applied that to our loved ones... imagine). We all have the right to the dignity of making our own choices. Whenever someone removes that, either through guilt or forcefulness, nothing positive comes out of it. The goal to being who you are naturally, is first to respect who you are naturally – then you will better be able to respect others and learn that ultimate rule of "mutually" consensual relationships. We as humans have made it a habit of breaking this boundary with not just nature, but with each other, and to ourselves. This is where psychologically, we have created a destructive pattern of being so busy with others' business, and who they are, that we have forgotten to handle our own business and addressing who we are. Think of any being out in nature, and you will find a supreme of example of self care, but self care that is respectful of others, I guarantee it.

Have you taken the time to really acknowledge the incredible parts of you without your status, salary, possessions?

There may be a point when our western society realizes that what we label as mental illness or a learning disability in many is merely one having a stronger sense to stay unique and not conform, and accelerated ability to stay in tune with one's natural senses and sensitivities.

"The real hopeless victims of mental illness are to be found among those who appear to be most normal." Many of them are normal because they are so well adjusted to our mode of existence, because their human voice has been silenced so early in their lives, that they do not even struggle or develop symptoms as the neurotic does.

They are normal not in what may be called the absolute sense of the word; they are normal only in relation to a profoundly abnormal society. Their perfect adjustment to that abnormal society is a measure of their mental sickness. These millions of abnormally normal people, living without fuss in a society to which, if they were fully human beings, they ought not to be adjusted."

~ Aldous Huxley

So, let's level with the caterpillar for real here. How long are we going to listen to someone else tell us what is best for our children, for our own bodies? Do we continue to try to "fix" what appears to be not normal rather than looking deeper to even define what "normal" is? Can we just admit that our status-quo society is no longer working, for anyone? And the main reason why is because it never includes nature's way of thinking and operating, and it continues to create discord and decline of our natural creative intelligent spirit that we as human beings were designed (by nature) to be. We can transcend past this simply by including nature in our thinking, and allow it to ripple into our own daily lives and outward towards others.

Do the events going on around you in the world seem "normal" to you? Is it really sensible to keep medicating kids without any clue what the long term effects will be on their brain development or bodies? What about our own bodies? How long do we continue to suck up the gerbil wheel lifestyle that has been fed to us that has now lived out it's cycle. It no longer rewards, and poses just as much risk if not more than if we create our own survival kit? And I am not just talking about our income, shelter, food, and protection, I am talking about our emotional survival – that part in our soul that keeps our spirit up and going, that feels and senses everything we need to know to guide our next step, words, movements, and creative decisions that determine our life path.

Nature constantly tugs us to breathe just like a mother feeds its child and does whatever it takes to keep their child alive. Whenever a person wonders about their place, that is the best place to start healing that hole, that numbness, that void inside – a deeper relationship with nature.

Whew.

You made it through all of that. This does get easier. As we explore the rocks of what is weighing us down, we can then discern and navigate our trail. The next chapter will break down quite a bit more, going down deeper into the rabbit hole in our situational assessment. I promise you, from my own journey of just facing it all, connecting the dots and creating strategies,, there is a lighter, more fulfilling road ahead.

Here is a simple feather and rock map. Try randomly placing circles with the thoughts that are either heavy near the rock in relation to how heavy they feel, and the size of the circle to express how concerning it is for you. Do the same with the feather area, where you feel lighter in hopeful thoughts. This gets you accustomed to the power of visual mapping, and inspired to create your own maps!

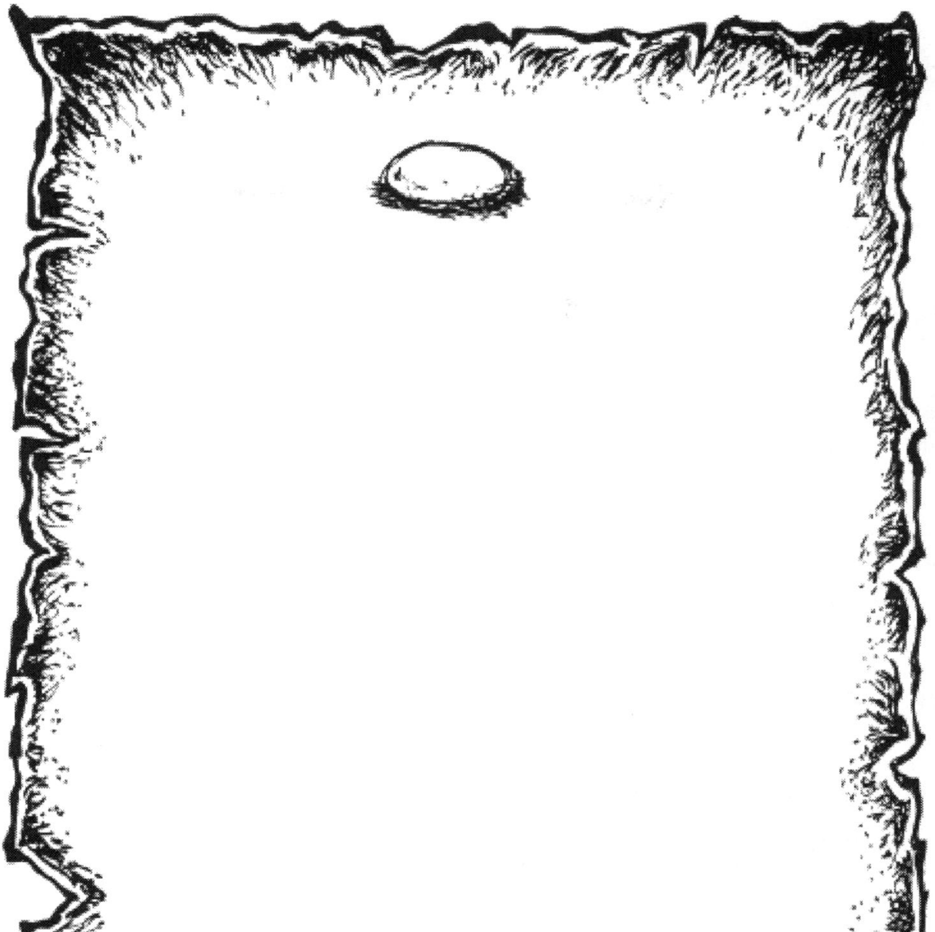

Shoes Optional ~ P. Hoke

I painted this while I lived in Florida form my favorite beach, as my reminder to take it easy on myself when I am faced with difficult challenges or truths.

CHAPTER 3

Down the Rabbit Hole

"But I don't want to go among mad people," Alice remarked.

"Oh, you can't help that," said the Cat, "we're all mad here. I'm mad. You're mad."

"How do you know I'm mad?" said Alice.

"You must be," said the Cat, "or you wouldn't have come here."

~ Lewis Carroll, Alice in Wonderland

If you're still with me after leveling with the caterpillar, congratulations. Many can't get that far, usually because of fear of the unknowns, or of the notion that there is intelligence in exploring other ways of thinking beyond our dominant linear thinking.

So, perhaps know that you were able to humbly face the world from caterpillar view, perhaps you would like to roll down the rabbit hole and connect some dots together. Shall we?

We must be mad as a species, otherwise we would not be where we are.

The quote above is referencing "mad," as crazy or insane here. Yet, I can attest, as I embarked on a deep dive into the trail of human stories, including the ones which became part of my own belief systems, and watched the impact of those stories on my life, the natural world, and the life of others, I not only saw the insanity of it all, I became actually mad. Like angry mad. How did we allow this and think it was going to be a responsible, ethical way to live? There is so much more to my last decade of connecting dots and unpacking, yet for here, the one thing I can attest is it has been liberating, enlightening, and I will never go back.

Amidst all the data and abilities literally right at our fingertips, here we are still feeling lost and arguing with each other about what to do. It doesn't take much to see how easily a story can be manipulated to ignite feelings to use as a method to divide, simply by playing on our fears.

I visualize a saying I heard a while back in one of my recovery groups that describes what it's like to reason with an addict still unaware of the plight of their addition: "It's like arguing about where to put the furniture on the Titanic."

In the movie Avatar, the native community measured one's insanity level by how connected they were with the natural world. If one was not able to feel and sense strong connections with natural elements, such as a tree or animal totem, then they were insane. These individuals were not excommunicated, however, but rather sent off with others who would try to work with them to see if they could be healed of the natural world disconnection. Now, let's really think about this from the most primal survival mindset. These communities were very aware that staying in tune with and connected to the environment that provided all that they needed to survive simply was common sense.

Thinking without creativity is, well, not fully thinking

E.O. Wilson, in his book, "The Social Conquest of Earth," references Paul Gauguin addressing the issues of religion and philosophy onto a canvas – where do we come from. What are we? Where are we going? "Humanity today is like a walking dreamer, caught between the fantasies of sleep and the chaos of the real world. The mind seeks but cannot find the precise place and hour. What have created a Star Wars civilization, with Stone Age emotions, medieval institution, and god-like technology. We thrash about. We are terribly confused by the mere fact of our existence, and a danger to ourselves and to the rest of life."

He goes on to state, "Conscious thought is driven by emotion; to the purpose of survival and reproduction, it is ultimately and wholly committed. The intricate distortion of the mind may be transmitted by the creative arts in fine detail, but they are constructed as though human nature never had an evolutionary history." He then goes on to address how much we have advanced sufficiently in technology now to begin to address our social evolution and begin the solutions. The solutions can be learned form insects..." We have no less to learn from the social insect, in this case to add background to the origin and meaning of humanity." Dr. Wilson embraces the creative arts as vital to our survival, with imagination as the source. Even in his incredible TEDTalk August 2012 to young scientists, he stresses to them to not allow a struggle with math to deter them from staying in the sciences, as science needs all talents, and they will find where they are needed in the field. This is so true, and the same goes for those who are naturally attracted to drawing, singing, dancing...and so on.

Random Art break...

My version of DaVinci's Virtuvian Man: just trying to make sense of this senseless imbalance caused by an old story from the dominant linear thinking, and still exists today, that somehow, women, the actual bearers of life, are ""secondary?"

Extreme Thinking

The current "group think" we are stuck in within most modern societies of this limited linear thinking has also led to our mind's need to compartmentalize everything. It has now arrived at the point that we end up feeling we must pick a "this or that," "right or wrong" story that leads to extreme thinking. It becomes our identity in our addiction to status and stuff, and now limits our ability to hold space for other's truths, pause and explore the fact that there are infinite combinations, infinite possibilities. Just looking at nature and the varied approaches in how it adapts depending on situations tells us the abundance of options, and that shifting our thinking it intelligently adapting. The extreme thinking has led us to cling to our limited lens, which perpetuates division, and my gosh, stress! Unnecessary stress that causes inflammation, which then causes us to be sick. Or, we run to our chosen form of "escape," whether it's misdirecting our anger, misdirecting our grief, or heading out for some "retail therapy" or other substance for relief. The facts are out that experiencing nature fully, experiencing creative processes (making things) offer that relief. Both also are proven to help us become more collaborative, meaning we are better able to hold space for multiple truths from multiple lenses. A mind relief that no money can buy, and relief to create a life we don't have to feel like we need to "escape." Wow.

Two ways the insanity keeps rolling along

So let's dive in and address two core elements of the insanity of the human species:

1. Our avoidance in addressing the thinking we are attached to, caused by the stories imposed upon us
2. Addressing the resulting apathy from our avoidance of looking at how these thinking patterns are not aligned with who we truly are as sensory intelligent, creative human beings connected to nature.

Both are fear-based. And this is not surprising considering our entire economic mindset is based on a scarcity mindset.

And if you don't think humanity has hit a new level of insanity, then I must kindly ask with the most caring heart, please try to create a trail of where you are in the human story and ways which might be buffering your mind from the realities of events happening outside your circle that are happening in live time? This is purely a gentle nudge as I had to do this myself. It took learning I had breast cancer to accelerate this exploration, and my hope is that you don't wait until a "force pause" to embark on your own journey down the rabbit hole of reality.

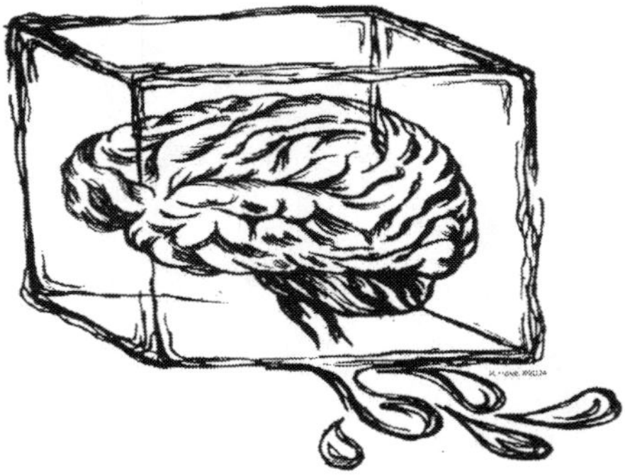

There is so much that stretches beyond the veils that have been placed over our eyes, at no fault of our, yet by an indoctrination of which we had no control over. Depending on our specific identities in relation to how our systems categorized us, our familial systems, belief systems, our teachers, the community in which we grew up in, how our parental figures were raised, our economic circumstances, whether we were in abusive environments or emotionally unsafe environments. We do now, however. You are here for one reason or another. It could be somewhere your arm was twisted into it, perhaps by me or someone who knows me. Or, that curiosity pulled you into this. Either way, here we are, and isn't curiosity fabulously exciting? I at many times resent now the saying "curiosity killed that cat." This, I believe is just one of the gazillion human made "stories" out that once again contributed to us fearing being curious. No, I refuse to believe that curiosity killed that cat, but rather, the cat either was not in its full awareness, plugged into its environment at the moment, or trusted something that was un-trust-able.

When I speak of giving ourselves permission to explore, I am referring to that mapping out the trail exercise. And yes, facing our addiction to status...that part of our conditioned brains that says to us: “Oh, is this going to be okay? What is so and so going to think?” I am pleased to let you know that the only “permission” you need to explore, learn or try anything is that from yourself. How do I know this? I look to any natural being. Simply by observing an insect, a bird, and mammal in action – they follow their attractions, period. They also listen to their distractions, which are actually natural attractions helping them survive, while that also are respectful of the general rules – or guidelines of the web of life. Respect and empathy is very much a part of that – something which our society has forgotten about, but we can see in many examples in nature, that these character traits for natural law are very much a part of the wiring we and all earth’s inhabitants are born with.

“It’s like ice formed around our hearts and minds keepings us so removed from our life source, our true selves, and each other. We have truly become a lonely species. It seems Earth is now melting this ice whether we like it or not”

- me

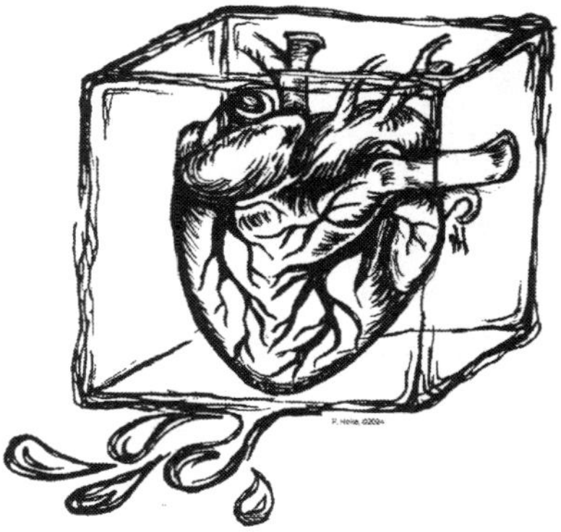

In most cases, with rare exceptions, the ones who lack them and breach these guidelines, learned to do so. So, all I ask, is follow your natural attraction to exploring the rabbit hole with me, otherwise, you may want to stop reading now. I'm not kidding. Just in case, I am going to repeat the quote at the beginning just as a reminder, so you don't come back to me saying, "Pam, you didn't warn me.."

"I can't go back to yesterday because I was a different person then."

~ Lewis Carroll, Alice in Wonderland

My deep wish is that more of us do become courageously curious like Alice, and can't go back to yesterday. Perhaps you might be able to, but I made a conscious decision that I simply wasn't satisfied with the way things were, and decided not to continue.

An excellent question arises in the book "Reconnecting with Nature," by Dr. Cohen: "Why historically, has the quality of the science we learn increased while the quality of air decreased?"

I don't know about you, but, this question is one that really jolted me. Did any of us really stop to think about this? Tells us a lot about how much we still do not know, but worse, tells us we are doing something very, very wrong, because we also have increasing violence, addictions, diseases, and more.

"To be a part of a system, a person, place, or thing must be in communication with that system. Earth is a global ecosystem and we are a part of it. Through natural attraction webstrings, Earth communicates with us, and all other being in supportive ways."

- Michael J Cohen

After reading this, my desire to fully participate the reality of how natural systems think, which are all around me is when I began my journey to natural self discovery. Starting with that restoring my relationship with it, learning to explore how it senses me, and how I sense it. Learning an entirely new language. Nature's language. I combined this with the language of art, which is shapes, textures, lines, color, light. Two languages which our human story has lost it's connection with. From now over ten years fulling plugging into these languages I have discovered not only who I really was, but as I pricked at the numb spots one by one, I began to feel more intelligent, more confident and compassionate. Both helped me face some extreme adversities, from fiscal losses from the mortgage crisis, breast cancer, loss of my spouse and mother in law from drug addiction, alcoholism and covid, into the ability to move forward into deep grief therapy, staying close with recovery friends, and onto digging deeper to truly go down the rabbit hole of why things are so messed so I could participate in changing things (hence the recent investment in graduate school studies).

The trails lead to some really messed up realities

Besides getting things all out of whack with regard to real priorities. Regarding our relationship with nature, it's like we have essentially walked right into our neighbor's house, grabbed whatever we wanted out of the fridge without even a thank you, let alone asked permission. And yet, we still walk around scratching our heads without addressing how intrusive, narcissistic, and harmful our lack of empathy for our life source we rely on to exist is.

Here are just a few of the mind traps which our limited modern linear thinking has created. Just a few to explore in a journal, perhaps? Also, this might be a moment to connect how our mind processes these, what our heart/body says compared to what nature might say.

Shaming and Blaming Cycle
Fear of Vulnerability
Fear of Ambiguity,
Change, Uncertainty, or Unknowns

Fear of what is "different" or not "normal"

We have adopted crafty ways of numbing ourselves to this core reality to the point that we have numbed ourselves as the pure, emotionally-driven beings we are, the natural beings that like Nature, are very much connected to every molecule in this universe and the fact that each time we breathe we are participating in the web of life – yet our human stories which continued to disconnect us from our life source and encouraged this numbing ourselves from truly experiencing, feeling the intimacy of this inborn connection with all of life, and recognizing it as the purest form of unconditional love that exists. Even some of the most amazing intellectuals and creatives who are working hard to develop solutions, seem to be missing this point – or, they touch on it slightly, yet never dive into that full feeling and sensory experience. It's like we are still just paying nature as our nurturer lip service. We are not fully walking "with" nature. We are merely touching the surface without creating that emotional connection. This is what biologists and even medical professionals have taught for years. To keep emotional distance from their subjects. Well the research is out, that only has caused more harm, because that "distanced" mindset has removed the very empathy which now every piece of research says is essential to intelligent, responsible care for people and planet, for how businesses, government and organizations need to operate effectively moving forward.

Just having to still have to talk about this, after decades

of knowing the reality can make anyone weary, and is understandable that so many have become ambivalent. It is getting tiresome to see this lip service coming from so many leaders, and even people in the profession who still are avoiding processing their own grief, their own anger so we can stabilize with nature's guidance to create effective strategies.. When we displace out un-checked grief, anger, frustration and lack of our own deep relationship to even sense how nature thinks, we are actually not effective and therefore hurting nature's voice. I find myself frustrated that there are some who work with wildlife are still in the dominant thinking that still keeps them at arm's length from nature's intimacy, that emotional connection at the deepest level. It is by fully letting nature into our psyche that we can disrupt the imbalanced linear thinking patterns and effectively communicate this urgent message. I am baffled that medical and psychology experts throw around the research of how walking in park helps, but continually diminish dedicated nature therapy that can be blended with art. Same goes for the art therapy world, that desperately needs to apply natural world connection as priority. My theory, based on my own personal experience of having to face the real me in nature, is that is part of the reason. Either way, we shall see.

Why we need to discover our natural self

Understanding the whole in our hearts sets us free. Current facts of the world:

After reading through multiple essays and articles quarreling back and forth about where the responsibility lies in a creating a cultural shift toward more earth-centered thinking, I decided to take a go at it from my experiences and from what I have observed.

We can, at this moment, any moment, stop the mind clutter and give ourselves permission to pause long enough so we can discover and create solutions to whatever ails us, or is stirring up our psyche. Nature is our personal, free therapist with endless examples of how to navigate life. It merely requires learning how to incorporate it into our thinking through identification and association with it daily. It takes practice.

The research is growing daily how nature increases endorphins, decreases stress levels, creative and cognitive thinking and overall enhanced sense of community and sense of belonging. Overall, the more access to nature improves overall health and well-being, yet why is it so hard for us to allow ourselves to create an intimate relationship with it? Our stories continue to view us a separate from it, when in fact, we are nature. We are organic beings. The only way is this story that we are separate from it, the story that we are superior over it, keeps us emotionally distanced enough for us to exploit it, destroy it, and therefore the continue the insanity of destroying ourselves in the process.

Nature gently and lovingly can become a guide on our unique journey of natural self discovery. It heightens our senses and sensibilities to come to conclusions we can trust in – but only if we let it fully "in."

Freeing the mind of our human clutter...

What I love most about the journey of natural self discovery is that it frees your mind of clutter by doing more of something. Think about it, most of your life, including most self help books from dieting to addiction therapy, you are generally told NOT to do something or less of it - causing that immediate inner shame, or bringing out that inner rebel inside. We all know this too well. Don't eat too much, drink, smoke... you can't do this or that. From the start we feel we are doing something wrong, causing that inadequate feeling...that "I'm mot good enough feeling.". I am going to do it wrong. I am bad, etc, etc. We don't have to accept or believe that is a positive way to start any journey. We grew up this way - hearing no or that we are doing something wrong. Mind you, this was all with good intentions, and yes, we all have to learn basic guidelines about a new skill, or general rule of consideration and conduct, however, somewhere along the path of humanity, we lost that respect for the uniqueness of an individual. So as a result, many of is live our life on a constant state of wondering if we are doing enough, doing it right, or just constantly questioning our path. This leads to a build-up of unworthiness, or just never feeling quite good enough unless we do, think, or approach life in a certain manner. Many of us seem to have that "something more" inside us. But what is that something more? How do we really know? Sometimes we rush to fill that feeling, and usually it is with the wrong medicine, person or group of people, or habit. Ok, enough negative for now, I am just trying to make the point, the case for a deeper connection with nature. Some of us think we are, I did for years – but I really didn't comprehend the depths of the ability to really plug into the communication system of nature, and how much, it would help my life path and overall health.

From here on out, we decide that we've had enough of this garbage, or toxic thinking swirling around to last several lives, and are now done with that mental game - it is counterproductive. This is basic psychology or what most experts call human nature. Sure, negative reinforcement works, but only in extreme cases - and very much exists in nature, yet the only way to lifelong habit is through positive reinforcement. There must be a reward. The reward of letting go of the negative beating we give ourselves, built in by the voices inside, is a renewed inner peace and confidence. The confidence comes from first acknowledging our innate, biological senses, and then working on the habit of trusting them.

Biology shows without a doubt we are each very unique, creative beings, through our DNA strands, fingerprints, and so much more.

No one can stop us from plugging back in, but ourselves.

What I strive to do here is help you begin to acknowledge that there are serious wounds inside all of us, even though they may not be obvious on the cover. The negatives, through our inner dialogue with ourselves, chip away at your heart - just like in a relationship where little hurts build up. They eventually erupt into that volcano of energy swirling around, and come out destructively in our behavior or worse, our physical health. The guarantee is if we aren't aware of inner selves and any negative or positive energy, science reveals that the energy must come out somewhere in some form. Energy is constant and must keep moving, and yes, like it or not, keep changing forms.

We then end up severed from our life source creating a void in our minds and hearts. This void is the absence of living and thinking with the very source that brings us life. If you can relate to either a ting of yearning to plug into natural beings like the indigenous people in the movie "Avatar" did, or relate to how Neo answered that nagging gut feeling to bravely take the red pill in the movie "The Matrix," then you have a good foundation of your natural sensory self, and what this amputation is referring to. If not, it's okay, because this book is pretty much helping to introduce this issue without blame, shame, or anyone ever feeling left out – just as nature works.

What happened to me after watching the movie Avatar, was that yearning to be able to "plug in" to nature like they did. And that is what made this movie so popular, and showed clearly our yearning to do so.

With the way our modern human systems and dominant thinking has evolved, we were denied any opportunity to create a real relationship with our inner nature by the best, most well-intentioned teachers. The dominant linear thinking separate from nature has conditioned to be indoors nearly 90% of our lives. We spend most of our days inside schools or offices, in cars, etc. and increasingly over time are primarily presented with the dangers of nature. This is the core of the void, because our inner nature yearns to be outdoors and bond with natural beings. We increasingly hurt more as we go about our days in western civilization where we have some really out of control habits, yet habits deep down inside we know are hurting and ourselves, and subsequently nature.

Try going into your bathroom and look at all the plastics bottles, think about the chemicals in those bottles, or go to your kitchen cupboard and not only see the mass of materials used to package your products, but look at the ingredients. Many of us adults, even me as an x-gener, can still recall being sent outside for the day and not to return until dark, I played in the dirt and drank from the garden hose. I loved to roll my lollipops in the dirt and lick them – well, that was me because I loved to see the reactions on my friend's faces. Now that I look back, however, perhaps my body was deficient of a mineral that was in that dirt.

The part of our dominant linear thinking that saddens me the most is now is that too many kids are being shoved medications to "contain" them in a non-natural environment, in particular, a non-creative environment. Or, the "disorder" label is thrown out there, when in fact, the research is growing that most simply have their sensory, conceptual language and ways of relating in tact - like that are actually immune to our current sick linear thinking.

The evidence is growing that all one has to do with a restless or unhappy child is get them outside for genuine nature exploration, experience, or even better, add an artistic experience outdoors such as drawing in the dirt. Allow them to get "messy," and explore, move their body around. A child and most teen's natural loves for nature and art are there...no wonder they are "acting up" or "acting out" as adults seeing they were denied these natural loves. Sorry, not rocket science here folks. Just ask Richard Louv or Sir Ken Robinson.

How to address our deprivation from our natural creative selves So, the hole in our hearts begins with this separation, a separation from what is natural. As our lives become more and more unsatisfying or difficult, the soul stirring begins.

"Every child is an artist. The problem is how to remain an artist once we grow up."

~Pablo Picasso

My heart sings every time I read this, as it is one of my favorite quotes by an artist. I had this posted behind my desk as an art teacher, and include in every one of my presentations during art workshops! I simply love what this quote stands for. It shows the genius within the artist Pablo Picasso, whether he was associating with the "growing up" part being our industrialized education or not, he taps on the beautiful realization that we lost part of ourselves in this, which causes the problem. The part I also love is when one thinks overall into the bigger picture of this – every child is an artist!

Meaning we were all born this way, and yes, science has proven that it is a competency we, and many other species are born with. Empathy is also innate to us and the natural world.

It is only because a dominant linear thinking system hijacked our natural thinking and relating. It has passed down for long so many of us heard that story that “we were not creative. We are all creative – it may not be in drawing or painting – it may be sculpture, or cooking, or designing homes, or creating the ideal educational platform, through music, theatre, dance...you name it. There is a creating ability in every one of us, and it mirrors the source of creation of life, the natural world. We just have to get back to giving ourselves permission to value and schedule in that discovery, exploration, and experimentation time as invaluable.

Just like you will never know how a specific food tastes unless you taste it, how the heck are you ever going to know which realm in creativity is within you, which one do you find you like and enjoy the most, unless you try it

I say this with love...no more excuses, and no more waiting around or saying it’s too late. I know people who pick up an instrument at 80 and play a tune within weeks, if they find they love it, it just comes naturally. There are people I have had in my watercolor workshops who picked up a watercolor brush for the first time, and the colors and strokes flowed so naturally, they kept doing it. It all depends on making that “leap” and trusting that it doesn’t matter what anyone else says or does... it is your journey of discovery, and no one else’s to judge, period. We also have to get past the placing “value” on the time spent doing creative endeavors. If a doctor told you today that if you did not start doodling or painting, or dance, or pick up a musical instrument, you would die in two weeks – would you listen to your inner creative spirit then?

It is time to value time spent in creative mode and time spent in nature as vital to our very survival, our whole being, our serenity, happiness, and physical well being. Just think about how great you feel after a nature or creative experience – the recharge effect, and increase brain waves should speak volumes on the validity or "value" to the point where you can ignore the societal mantra now, and know and trust that the escape is the best medicine for health and intelligence you could ever give yourself.

"There is no economy without nature, or healthy people who can make or buy things. The sooner we align with nature's economy, the sooner we have a chance towards a responsible, sensible existence on Earth."

- me

"Paradoxically, what keeps the so-called consumer society going is the fact that trying to find yourself through "things" that are not aligned with our natural human-ness doesn't work.

It only temporarily satisfies a physical dimension that on the surface.

Yes, we need housing, clothes, furniture, tools, transportation. Yet we can learn a thing has Being-ness, a temporary form that has its origin from nature...the source of all things, all bodies, all forms.... When you live in a world deadened by mental abstraction, you don't sense the aliveness of the universe anymore.

Most people don't inhabit a living reality, but a conceptualized one."
~ Eckhart Tolle, A New Earth

Now, there's the statement that pulls in The Matrix movie for me. Most have created their own matrix, an illusion of life with things, yet not sensing those things as actual living molecules that, we ourselves, actual living molecules share with the entire universe. Somewhere we lost this vital cord to our soul, and that is what is creating that something is missing feeling. So, what this book is about, is getting that feeling back inside. It is not about giving up things, yet embracing them to find a realistic balance, primarily the balance in your own psyche so that you are better equipped to make decisions that are truly based in reality, and therefore not part of the sand castle reality society has created that will, as we all saw this past year from Hurricane Sandy and from our continued joblessness, will get swept away – leaving us sad, but could also leave us helpless. This book is about helping ourselves, and learning all those survival instincts that many believe are like a rocket science novel that you now have to watch survival shows to understand. Yet, we have survival senses, we can smell our surroundings, we have all the abilities that we need, and more.

What I sense is many of us are dying inside emotionally because of the corner we have painted ourselves into a corner. And even with the research and date out, actionable solutions developed and available, the fear story of ambiguity, of the unknowns, the unfamiliar trails still keeps us from making authentic leaps.

It's like society has now deemed simple, such as a preposterous claim that "just" incorporating a habit of immersing in nature and art experiences cannot possibly be valid – we have to complicate and over-think everything. This is just like over-painting an oil painting – it will get muddy in color eventually. This is not some voodoo, it is not tree hugging, and it certainly does not involve rituals, chants, or pretending to fit-in with others by saying or doing things we may not fully believe, or anything that one does not find naturally attractive as an individual. Studying and acknowledging the depths of our psychological and physiological connection with nature and our natural creative abilities is no longer something we, as a collective society growing into a collective madness, can no longer ignore.

It is our life source, and is at the end of the day, the only truth we as individuals can fully trust in because we can "feel" it. And if we must refer to research here, time and time again, beyond the studies that continuously arise regarding our disconnection with nature, lack of innovative, conceptually strategic thinking, is the increasing lack of empathy. They correlate to the point where these aspects of society are creating a perfect storm. As empathy for and inclusion of nature decreases, a focus on artificial things, violence, destruction of other natural beings, and depression increases.

Isn't it odd that in one article, an author will breeze through a positive note about talking a walk in the park is great medicine, then the same author will move onto how wonderful their new sports car is. I've watched environmentalists trying so hard to get their message out through from caring for animals to climate change, I see climate scientist, biologists, ecologists out there struggling to show how understanding more through research is the answer, I see psychologists continue to re-invent new forms of "talk-therapy," I see doctors and medicine specialists constantly switching their theories about what is good for us and what is not, I see psychiatrists constantly testing new medicines in search for that magic "pill," however, I have yet to see anyone immerse in full conscious contact studies with nature and the creative experience as necessary to hack our addiction to our current thinking systems.

It is the root that is causing the inner conflict, discontents and overall dissatisfaction in today's lives in civilizations. We are taught and rewarded financially to think in a dominant linear mindset, which is the complete opposite of our natural way of knowing reality. Yet, we are conditioned to answer however society tells us to, fearing we might lost our status or stuff.

Our story of status and stuff.

So, how might we overcome the fear just enough to create a strategy that focuses on the strengths of our natural selves in relation to our unique contribution to our world? Research shows over and over we are motivated through purpose. Dan Pink has written about this, and has been speaking about his for decades. Check out his book "Drive," and our need for autonomy, mastery and purpose. You can also search "Dan Pink, motivation, Ted Talk" on YouTube. One of my favorite TedTalks ever, right there next to Mel Robbins' "How to stop screwing yourself over," and Brene Browns' "Vulnerability Ted Talks. In general, yes, I highly encourage if you aren't already, create a healthy addiction to watching TedTalks.

What about purpose?

And when you look at the latest trends in the job market, most job seekers, especially young millennial and genZ, are choosing work that aligns with their values and purpose, even accepting less pay in order to live in their purpose and something meaningful.

When we really embark down the rabbit hole, exploring all lenses, taking time to really hearing, and FEELING, how others from completely different backgrounds we can grasp a deeper sense of how our human stories passed through generations has created a dysfunctional mess within our societies today. Back to the Titanic story, we keep arguing about where to move the furniture rather than addressing the reality at hand. The ship of humanity is heading for trouble, not earth. Earth is simply being Earth and regenerating herself. And either we as a collective family can learn to work as a functional, sensible family in a shared plight to adapt and evolve, or it is we that perish. Earth will just keep going. So my point here, is the issue I take with climate communications, environmental messaging: stop patronizing Earth by saying we are "stewards." This implies the very human superiority complex which we must get over if we are truly going to create a healthier relationship with our planet. E.O. WIlson's book titled the "Social conquest of Earth" makes it abundantly clear that we are not in charge, Earth is. Yes, we continue this narrative that somehow we just need to continue this disconnected, arm's length, guilt-trip approach like Earth is some fragile child. When do we really pause and investigate deeper into why the messaging, amidst all the scientific data and facts, continues to fall on deaf ears? Perpetuating the divide and conquer tactic, and blaming and shaming is simply not working. Why? Because of this way of infantatlizing Earth, all natural beings in a way which disrupts the whole "getting right-sized" and developing a healthier relationship with nature is the key.

We are still tokenizing nature, making it look as woo. Forest bathing, and all these amazing movements are fabulous, yet when do we stop presenting it as "woo." The same happens when in the artistic creation experience.

Our disconnect from each other purely in the inability to walk in other's shoes (have true "empathy" rather than "sympathy), mirrors our disconnect form nature and our inability to walk in nature' shoes and do our best to envision how nature experiences how we treat it.

When we being to feel like we really do fit in just perfectly on Earth In my opinion, the only path to genuine and effective "live in harmony with Nature as much as possible, yet continue to participate and interact in healthy ways with world, which is, the reality of our communities of today.

The over-consumerism, addictions, hurtfulness, and cut-throat nature-destroying, and oppressive systems which are purely based on a scarcity mindset which is no longer serving any of us, actually is harming all of us. Harming our physical health, our fiscal health, our mental and spiritual well-being. Even economists of today are unpacking in collaboration with sociologists, psychologists and even referring to the sci-fi creators whom were the most accurate in predicting what is currently happening right before us. A book that truly opened my eyes was from my MPA studies was the book "Farsighted," by Steven Johnson. This takes on a journey of how it is the poets, philosophers, artists, writers, who have historically more accurately predicted, and created the most effective solutions than the most revered intellectuals. It also shows how strategic conceptual mapping, with many minds to assure multiple perspectives, is proven to be the most effective tool is facing any challenge or dilemma.

Many of my guru marketing friends (many who are extremely dissatisfied with your lives) have been describing today's society and communications landscape as the "YOUniverse." There is a trend of hyper-individualism that has completely taken over, yet the marketers, politicians and media love capitalizing on it – as long as they stir the discontent, then encourage that self-contentedness to the extremes by telling people how much they "deserve" this or that – this addictive behavior will continue.

Ditching the stories that no longer serve us

So, now what? Here is an interesting way to determine if you really are ready to explore how deep the rabbit hole goes, if you really can find a part of you that is attracted to a heightened level of consciousness with your natural self. This means, a deeper connection with nature. I am not talking about the talkers, or those who work with nature or animals, or in medicine who think they are connected...not at this level. This is what could be considered plugging into nature just as the indigenous tribe members do in the movie Avatar. It is very similar to those who take the red pill in the movie The Matrix. The reason I say this is not to shock, but to share the reality as I experienced it...and it is just that, reality. It's like Morpheus in The Matrix says, "You can take the blue pill, and go back to believing whatever you want to believe, or, you can take red pill, and I can show how deep the rabbit hole goes." All I can tell you personally, my friends, is that once I read and resonated what I wanted to accept and deal with what I could deal with one baby step at a time, I feel so much better – each day feels so much more rewarding, and like the quote by Alice " I could never go back." But, that's just me. I am, essentially, only offering the truth I experienced, and a means to guide you to your own truth – and trust me, in this ride with Nature, you get to make up your own mind, follow your natural attractions, and relax and let Nature support and guide you.

An interesting early experience in my art teaching days.

It was initially an obstacle as a high school art teacher to be "allowed" to simply take my students outside to draw, and the system made it so difficult to take the kids on a trip to a park or anywhere outside the school walls. What is most baffling, is that the students become so conditioned to be indoors, they initially have a hard time to adjusting to even the thought of being outdoors. They have a difficult time interacting with the real thing because they are so accustomed to nature experiences through books, the Internet and movies to the point that even touching a tree seems strange and foreign to them. And sadly, especially as they get older, they simply block out that innate need and develop a preference to be indoors. I pulled my daughter out of her school to home-school due to her school principal taking away recess time, stating to me she was only required by Florida state to have the students outdoors a required amount of hours, of which they get in physical education. My daughter came home that day upset because gym class was indoors due to rain. Fed up is what I was – I really try to give our education a chance, but with regard to my kids... well, I will not put up with their natural selves being squashed to that extent, so that make me what I call "circumstance home-schooler," if the circumstances are not best for my child, then I fix it as my responsibility to them as any mother has those instincts even in the natural world.

I rest my main case

If you have made it this far, thank you! We went down quite the rabbit hole together! You made it through the heaviest part of this book, and now the chapters will be shorter.

My hope is there is plenty here to prove the absolute necessity to relearn direct conscious contact with our life source and the creative intelligence it holds, is essential to living. The more of us bring this into our minds and disrupt the old story loop that is perpetuating harm upon ourselves, each other and our planet, the better chance we've got! Besides, if you are feeling like me, I can at least feel better about how I am walking along the planet through the time I get to have here.

Almost through our "Pause" phase! The last stop during our will be exploring the true depths of this "natural creative sensory intelligence" I keep mentioning.

Who's Story is It? Activity

The Lighten Up Trail Map might assist in processing and discerning your thoughts/stories from which are truly naturally yours, or someone else's story that was booted up like software. Going to nature somehow (natural area, plants or pets), sitting quietly. Try making a list of what you want, or want to do, or have always wanted to do - and listen for the "shoulds" or "should not" stories. Which feel mis-aligned with your true self?

Lighten Up Trail Map | Natural Self Discovery, copyright 2024

Mother Raven with Moon ~ *P. Hoke*

This is a Raven who I get to encounter at a local beach area, and she always smiles at me. I love full moons because they keep me connected with nature's reliable intelligent cycles that keep life going.

CHAPTER 4

Natural Intelligence

"Look deep into nature, then you will understand everything better."
~ Albert Einstein

The statement above is true, however you will never grasp the depths of what Einstein is referring to until you place value in your modern-wired brain to indulge. If you begin to really take time out to sense and feel deeply with nature, and think with nature, more often you really will understand things better. Your brainwaves increase, the endorphins release making you not only feel great, but more creative, and yes, more intelligent. The beauty of the endorphins releasing is that making mental nature connecting a habit (no one has to know unless you share it with them), is that others do become more tolerable – meaning yes, you can become more patient. Mostly, because you become more like nature, and know it may be a waste of time or inefficient to exert any mental or physical energy for an annoying or toxic person nearby.

"Do you think I've gone round the bend?"
"I'm afraid so. You're mad, bonkers, completely off your head. But I'll tell you a secret. All the best people are."
~ Lewis Carrol, Alice in Wonderland

Now we finally get to plug into what really is reality. And the reality of the dominant form of thinking that modern humanity has glued itself onto. We are literally so addicted to this now, our brains fire off alarms whenever we do try to think conceptually, collaboratively (with nature and other cultures), or gosh forbid, curiously!

Our conditioning has told us to say after a refreshing day in the park, vacation (which travel statistic show usually involves the natural, real world): "oh, now I have to go back to the real world." Really?

Which "reality" is real? I think by now we can answer this honestly. I find myself chuckling inside when I hear that phrase now, only because now I know what is real, and what was made up by humans.

So the first question is: Are you convinced at this point that you were born naturally creative and intelligent?

Next question: Are you convinced that this is a necessary element for all of us to adapt as a species?

If not, may I guide you back to Chapter1 – lather, rinse and repeat until it sinks in...you were biologically born with nature's inherent intellect, sensory abilities, and creative adaptation capacities.

5 minutes a day outside sitting quietly, or even better, volunteering at the nearest wildlife or marine life rescue

organization to get closer. The largest point to get across to you in this chapter is this: when you balance using your whole brain, you instantly become more creative and intelligent.

Using your whole brain is balancing all aspects of it, the left side, the right side, staying active in the emotions buried within through your dreams, and most importantly, realizing that we all have the duality of New Brain society thinking and the long lost ways of ancient nature-centered wholeness, healing, intuitiveness and wisdom residing in our minds before our modern dominant thinking systems took over.

Do you really know all the capacities and senses you are born with? Some may call this common sense or instinct, but the reality is, these are very much a vital part of our very being, and by not using these capacities, we are completely short changing ourselves and our ability to find true happiness.

What I am introducing is not necessarily something new, it is ancient wisdom. And, not that I am diminishing all the incredible fields of study and organizations who help open our minds to help us tap into our creative genius, but, personally, I had to find a way that was not cluttered with terminology or philosophical jargon that only complicates things for me.

Perhaps it is the artist in me, where I live in a more visual and emotional world, but all I know is my quest was to find simple ways that weren't clinical or confusing. This opens the doors to the creativity and wisdom on how nature keeps itself going. It's like learning to have that "knowing" from sensing, similar to how the clouds "know" or sense, when to release rain, how a gecko "knows" - senses to grow a new tail, or how a spider "knows" - senses to spin a web in a certain way.

When you plug into the planet mentally, you are plugged back into the universe and the genius, the creative intelligence and love that keeps the entire system going. Nature's language is one that we already know, we feel it in our gut all the time, we just have to re-learn it because our human-language and intellectual filters have taken over. The freedom is truly exhilarating, and it actually is an experience one can become addicted to.

The creatively intelligent design of your entire being can be found in nature. Sensing and Valuing your natural CREATIVE self within : Nature's measure of intelligence: survival capacity: ingenuity, awareness of all senses and adaptability

I met the most intelligent, brilliant minds in my art classroom at the high school. And guess what? They were all labeled as ADD, ADHD, gifted (meaning social difficulties) or rebellious. Once they had a non-language way of expression, a way that was not dictated or spoon fed, they flourished not only in the art room, but in their math, language arts and sciences. Research is proving this time and again – and it is quite baffling how our education system and parents continually talk about it, but won't do anything about it in a genuine way. Why? Because of fear: fear of ambiguity again, or calling things our for what they are as many know, causes us to lose comfort in our status or with our stuff. I love that more and more of us are getting brave to exit the "comfort" zones and ruffle feathers - especially to do what is right by our kids, They need to learn how to face an empty space, an empty canvas, and empty piece of paper as an exploration of their whole mind and sensory language, not fear it. The same goes for us adults! How will we ever show them if we are not doing it ourselves?

The most potent way to grasp your natural creative genius is to fully acknowledge and experience each and every one of your natural born senses. There are many more than five, contrary to what you were taught in school. Creative instincts are natural intelligences, and yes, humans being born to create, are natural creators! That means you. And if we look back to cave drawings, arr is a universal language, and reveals what cannot be translated in our limited "word" minds.

"Art" is any outward expression of creativity within, in all mediums from writing, making something unique, arranging things, solving a problem, painting, sculpting, dance, music, cooking, parenting, gardening, building a shelter, and beyond.

An "artist" is anyone, or being who freely engages in expression of creativity from within, either for enjoyment or survival. This can be someone who creates a beautiful dinner, a sculpture, a music score, or even a spider that creates an innovative web based on the available branches and leaves surrounding it.

My definition of "talent" is when one is passionate about something and it feels natural doing it. One can naturally be good at doing something, yet may not be passionate about it, and one can be passionate about something yet does not feel natural doing it. Discovering one's talents is knowing and feeling both natural attractions when doing something. The key for anyone is to try anything, everything, giving all activities a full chance to sense your attractions, then trust in what you feel about the results (not what another says, or would say about it).

Tapping-into nature by tuning-out the human clutter

In order to really begin to "tap in," you can begin learning how to "tune out" the human language clutter and stories you tell yourself. And yes, it means turning off the earpods while running outdoors so you can tune-into nature's sounds and sense all of it fully. Being fully present, just as you would issue another human if you were meeting with them. Tapping in means staying in the tactile, sensory world, which means try to stay with actual drawing pads for notes - there is a science behind this where our senses become more ignited with the actual pressures and textures, the transfer of ink to paper, or pencil to pen. There are chemical reactions that occur, and actual sensory stimuli which positively impact t the experience.

Retail therapy. We find ourselves seeking joy in shopping, acquiring new artificial things that destroy the earth – we love money, we become addicted to a power-over mentality of being "better then" others – yet, this all requires ignoring what these behaviors do to the earth. It's like we are having an illicit affair. We turn that blind eye and find our inner justifications that we are just trapped, it's hopeless. I still find myself running to this odd behavior even in my plight for nature! Or running to escape into an episode of Outlander on Netflix, or a bag of potato chips. Augh! My pause button (I had one tattooed one on my arm because I know I will forever need a reminder to pause and do a mind, body with the natural world reality check. I still choose to do the "things," yet I consciously decide with the pause, reflect, respond method first, so at least I discern and strategize knowing the consequences. I accept the gradual process of navigating the modern humanness with my natural humanness, and there is a whole heck of a lot of messy in-between all that! Sound weird? Yes. Well, we humans are weird, yet nature made us brilliantly, curiously, and creatively weird.

There is good news...as we learn to unplug from our mind clutter of our the human-centric stories we hear from others and tell ourselves...even for just a few minutes a day, we get that little vacation of the mind, we feel some relief, and begin to heal our personal relationship with the which we inherently love, gives us life, and brings us joy...our relationship with Nature.

I experienced this gradual healing process. The guilt started to fade away, and I felt hope just by allowing myself to be closer to Nature mentally. I began making small, realistic changes... and each time I did, I felt a joy within swell. There is a wordless fulfillment from this exchanging love with Nature – I call it creating "peace of nature for my peace of mind."

The need to create...

We have it in us, we have just been taught that it is a luxury, time not "productive." This is the same story we are sold regarding spending time in nature. My challenge to all industries is creativity be valued in all disciplines because without it, there is no moving forward. My challenge to all industries is to add the Nature ingredient, because with Nature, well, we do not live. (Not rocket science here, folks.)

We can normalize the strange, the "weird," the unusual of courageous, curious, creative exploration. We actually need to at this point.

Here are some incredible insights from one of my favorite "Creative Crusaders", Daniel Pink:

"We crave to create, there is a reason…survival."

- Dan Pink

"While complying can be an effective strategy physical survival, it's a lousy one for personal fulfillment. Living a satisfying life require more than simply meeting the demands of those in control. Yet in our offices and our classrooms we have way too much compliance and way too little engagement. The former might get you through the day, but only the latter will get you through the night."

"The monkeys solved the puzzle simply because they found it gratifying to solve puzzles. They enjoyed it. The joy of the task was it own reward."

I know I am not alone in this journey. I see and hear it every day in news, TV when I watch it. I have read about this yearning in some of the many amazing books I have read over the years, in particular the ones addressing the push for creativity and imagination. The rumbling, the tension has been going on for quite some time, especially as our generations begin to answer that tension within them that gives them the courage to speak out about the importance of creativity in humans. Our education system is leaving children behind...all of them because it is not nurturing that inner natural creative spirit. It gets squashed very early on because it does not fit into the modern agenda. Why? Because creativity is part of our inner nature, and part of that inner nature is communicating with nature, a language which does not have words, numbers or labels at its core. There is no denying it – and, of course when it is squashed there will be the consequence of inner conflict. The tension-release relationship law of nature tells us very clearly that only bad things happen when things get off balance.

Sure, as our brain grows, the brainwaves connect throughout = and it all eventually comes together. But, how can we achieve genuine "whole mindedness?"

Einstein is our best example of this because his brain was weighed, and unlike all the other scientists and philosopher's brains, his weighed exactly the same on both sides. The others, well, they all were "left" heavy – the left, analytical side, that is. Einstein spent his life using both sides of his brain. I learned this when I was about 17 years old, and have been striving to do the same – nurture both sides of my brain. Why? Because they are there!

I loved playing around in the right side of the brain, and learned that this made me do better in all subjects thanks to Betty Edwards' "Drawing on the Right Side of the Brain." Now that I mention this book, I must add here quickly a note to all fellow art teacher out there: stop saying you aren't getting any "talented" kids to work with. Get this book, embrace it, and learn that part of your role is to help them all nurture their right brains – all that has happened to the ones who don't seem to do well in art class is they haven't been given permission to tap into that side and play. And worse, once they have on negative experience of someone else telling them how to do it (which contradicts the core of an individual's unique creative journey), their enthusiasm to even try is squashed. An art teacher's job is to at least show a student they have it in them – it may not be something they become passionate about, but it is in them. This is where Ken Robinson comes in, another of my favorite "Creative Crusaders." I read his book "The Element" early on during my design business time, after the teaching experience - it made so much sense to the state of our modern-mind-led creative squashing process that was happening in both homes everywhere and schools.

In Robinson's introduction of "The Element," he so boldly tells the beautiful story of an elementary art class where a young girl was asked what she was drawing by her teacher. The girl says, "I am drawing a picture of God." The teacher says, "But nobody knows what God looks life." The girl said, "They will in a minute."

Robinson goes on..."I love this story because it reminds us the young children are wonderfully confident in the own imaginations. Most of us lost this confidence as we grow up. Ask a class of first graders which of them thinks they are creative and they'll all put their hands up. Ask a group of college seniors this same question and most of them won't" Sigh. This reality I so clearly felt in my first years teaching high school art. Some took the class just to fill in credits with the hopes it would not hurt their GPA, some took it because there was no other place to go, and some took my class because their friends did. Only about 20 percent where there because they genuinely enjoyed art, and had persevered somehow their confidence in creating, the rest, well, we all know, art seemed like a great place to screw around, because we were taught to believe it wasn't "valuable" or a "valid" activity – anymore that spending time in nature was "valuable" or "valid." Well, thank goodness we now know the reality is we were dead wrong all along – and that both of these activities are very much part of our souls, keep us sane, and helps us to use our full brain capacity and keeps us feeling human beings!

Ken Robinson really hits the nail on the head when he makes this startling point that made my heart sing when I read it, "I believe passionately that we are all born with tremendous natural capacities, and that we lose touch with many of them as we spend more time in the world. Ironically, one of the main reason this happens is education. The result is that too many people never connect with their true talents and therefore don't know what they're really capable of achieving. In a sense, they don't know who they really are."

So, just as the Cultural Creatives grow, so does the "Rise of the Creative Class" by Richard Florida drive home the case for creativity. Yet another Creative Crusader on my favorite list.

"The wealth generated by the creative sector is astounding. It accounts for nearly half all wage and salary income in the United States. Still, we have not even begun to tap into our creative potential. Human creativity is a virtually limitless resource. Every human being is creative ins some way.... creativity is the great leveler. It cannot be handed down, and it cannot be "owned" in the traditional sense. It defies gender, race ethnicity, sexual orientation, and outward appearance." Richard Florida

Florida finds the real challenge is to level the disruption the growing shift to creative is causing. From this, he does extensive research on where creatives are living, he exhausts to discover the answers to help the shift occur, because it is so vital for survival. He also points out that there is increasing drug addiction, postponed or ended marriages in this field, for example. This tension, which is natural when you look to the natural world regarding any change, may be due, in my opinion, simply because society tends to resist change – those who work in creative fields still feel this tension, some inner conflict. I know, I have been one my entire life – back to that misfit feeling, but sort of kind of now fitting in because creativity is cool. Just like being a computer nerd is way cool. However, there is still a tension and stirring that no one can seem to pinpoint – a stirring I've been trying to figure out, even as my design boutique boomed in 2001, once my nerdy computer geek of a husband and I teamed up and made over

$120,000 our first year in business during this creative boom. (And oh yes, we were not prepared, and has the tax bill to show it, and the spiral that ensues from self-employment – but, that's another book of the reality that our country still is not about embracing the 90% of small businesses, which are the really small mom and pops like mine).

That stirring, to me, is that even though Florida is striving to embrace the "infinite" creativity, there is still the focus on the money, the wealth...the capitalization of it. I do believe this is where the pressure came in, and creativity is a natural process. It cannot be "robotized" as I felt in the few ad crank out shops, and even when I was swamped with about 15 brand identities to do in one week if we wanted to pay that new mortgage we were facing. Augh! So, more on that point later, the main thing is how creativity is now extremely important to our society as it evolves. I will move later on onto how, like Nature, we cannot take dominion over creativity, it is impossible to control it, and certainly not force it to emerge out any faster than we would expect an oak tree to seed – but, as our modern society dictates, we feel compelled to find a way to harness it. Now, imagine if all out-of-work, or unhappily employed individuals at this moment genuinely tapped back into their creative genius...do you think they would continue in their fruitless attempts to impress someone or a corporation once they realized they really could create a life they wanted and be their own boss? Doubtful.

"Unless someone like you cares a whole awful lot,
Nothing is going to get better. It's not."

- Dr. Seuss, The Lorax

Daniel Pink begins with a profound statement, "This book describes a seismic – though as yet undetected – shift now under way in much of the advance world. We are moving form an economy and a society built on the logical, linear, computer-like capabilities of the Information Age to an economy and a society built on the inventive, empathic, big-picture capabilities of what is rising in its place, the Conceptual Age."

He goes on to beautifully describe in detail how he receives a brain MRI and a series of tests so he can see his brain, and reveal the realities of the recent research which as he says, "the right hemisphere today has achieved a measure of legitimacy, It's real,. It's important. It helps make us human. No neuroscientist worth her PhD ever disputes that." He continues in intellectually weighing out all the research on the brain, yet to come to the vital conclusion in the scope of reality of society – our creative part, our right brains, need to be nurtured and valued fully in order for us to be "whole." He is correct – and I so love how this biological point hits the message home clearly. Now, let's add our natural intelligences (our natural senses) to the equation... now our brains are on bursting with an entirely new level of responsible, healthy intelligence far beyond what out human textbooks, or computers could ever reach.

Nature is the creative source, the ultimate Muse

Creating a deep connection with nature beyond a surface, "oh that is so pretty," mindset opens the floodgates to creativity, purely because of it's sensory buffet. It is how we fully achieve using our whole minds. Plug into our natural creativity, our natural selves, by plugging into nature. As I quote everywhere... from the man who successfully used both sides of his brain, remaining fully plugged into nature, and the arts as a violinist.

"Look deep into Nature, then you will understand everything better."

- Albert Einstein

So there you have it! Congratulations, you made it through the long "pause" phase of absorbing and beginning to process a lot of truths. Now it gets a bit easier, as we move into the reflect phase where we connect the dots of all this and start making some sense of it all.

Activity: Let Nature unleash your creativity

To truly arrive into a natural creative state (the zone, which feels like meditation, yet better), we need to let go of the left brain (human language, modern society) barriers – remove the clutter of human language. Letting loose like is easy by simply following your natural attractions in nature and simply feeling them without attaching any labels. The goal is to focus on the sensory feelings – those gut reactions to the colors, textures, elements around you in the moment.

Unchain yourself from creative barriers. Grab your nature journal and find your nature space.

Sit quietly where you feel most welcomed, where your natural senses assure you it is safe and comfortable. Remember, nature does send you signals if there is something going on that may not work, just stay aware and open to the signals with your nature intelligence.

Begin to just enjoy and sense the shapes, textures, and colors beyond, and just scribble shapes. No specific direction – knowing there is no one standing over you to judge what comes out. Keep adding to the scribbles, almost coloring in parts. After a while, you will feel new visual ideas.

Now, start thinking of your goals in life, and slowly bring in words into your scribbles. Jot down the new ideas that come to mind. This activity of just sitting with nature and randomly scribbling and coloring is great for when you are feeling stagnant – the motion of just putting shapes on paper and allowing your mind to flow freely from the visual and sensory inspirations from nature will invigorate, awaken and engage the firing of new, unused neurons in your brain. This helps bring about solutions that are not possible with just the linear left brained language thought process we have been accustomed to. You are using your "whole brain" when you let go and dive into the non-language, natural realm of thought. This is the space, the zone that many artists, dancers, musicians, naturalists, and all creatives speak of. Many today are still not fully acknowledging or are aware that most of this is inspired directly by nature – with repetitive contact in sensing all parts of the full non-verbal communication with nature, anyone, can expand their thought horizons and creative ideas and solutions. It is just a matter of creating that mental space and time habitually - prioritizing it as a matter of life and health to you and your journey here on earth.

List all of your creative qualities out in this area too! You will be amazed where you are utilizing your creative capacities in life and how to grow and nurture them. Acknowledging them and embracing them is the first step!

The two books which also helped me unleash my creativity, and artist within are "Drawing on the Right Side of the Brain" by Betty Edwards and "The Artist's Way" by Julia Cameron. I will be referencing these amazing life-changing books more later. And I would not be a good creative friend if I did not strongly recommend the expert at nature connected art, Bob Ross! He understood kinship with nature as our friend, and ultimate

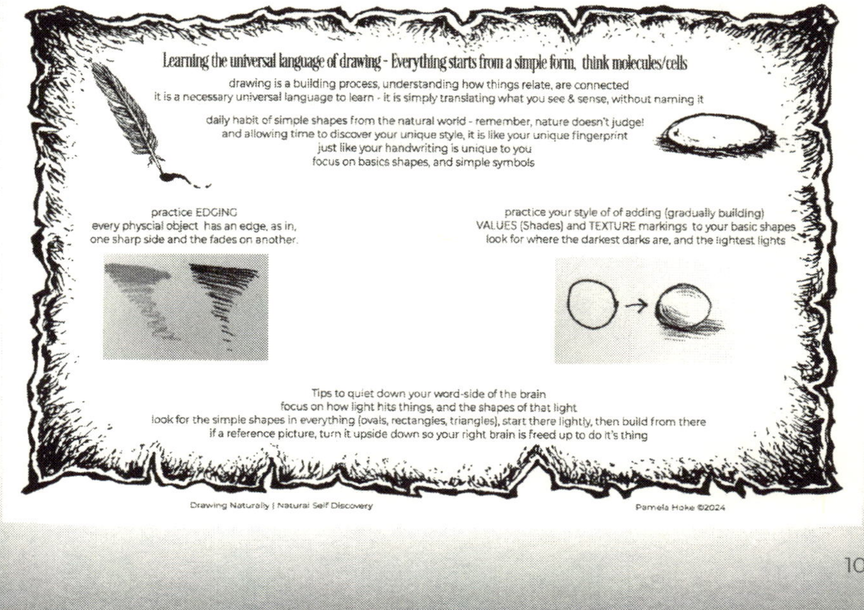

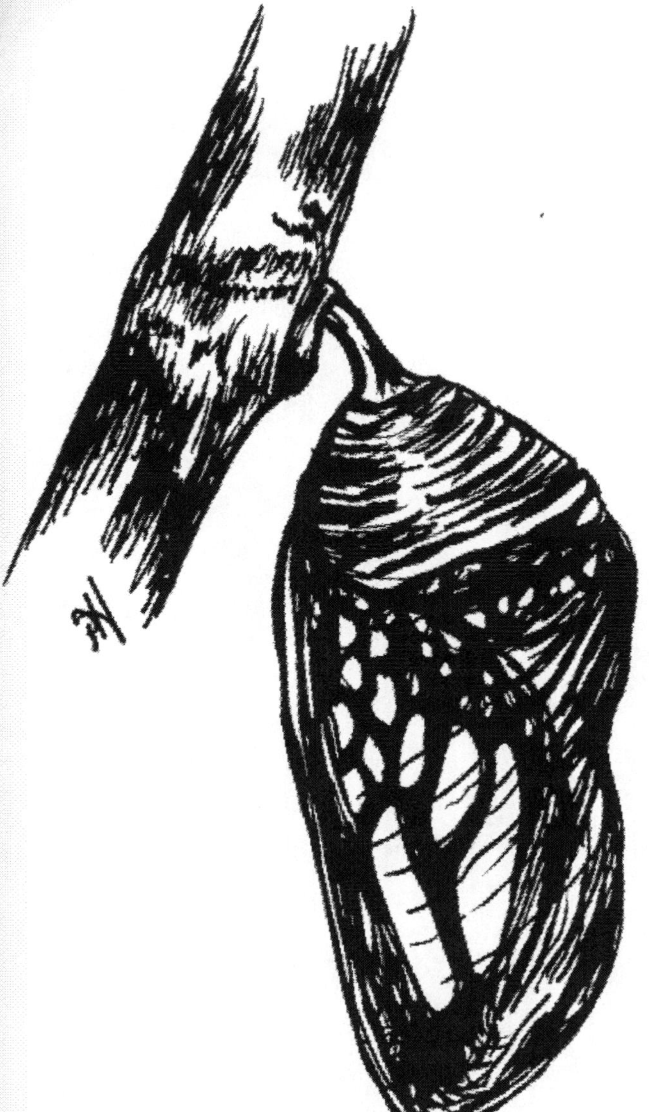

PHASE 2

REFLECT

The space to notice what a situation or relationship is reflecting to us, gather more information and lenses to expand our perspective, understanding and options

Young Cow at Full Moon ~ P. Hoke

I had the priviledge of meeting his magnificent young lady, just about a year old, at my friend's local island farm.

CHAPTER 5

We're just Babies

We can learn to go beyond the stories, beyond just seeing to fully sensing, and thinking with our life force.

"You're just a baby!" the native woman screamed at him.

- from the movie, Avatar.

Maturity as species

As I mentioned clearly on the back cover of this book, nature simple would not think we are behaving maturely. After our long journey in the first four chapters, now we are merely going to ride through processing it all and connecting some dots so we can better create a strategy moving forward. An efficient, responsible, sensible, and enjoyable trail forward. And yes, more mature - aligned in our natural purpose and needs, aligned with others and most importantly, aligned with our life source,...as our driving life force!

Earth is the Life Expert

Heightened awareness Knowing and acknowledging your Natural attractions - secrets to a happier path
It's time to get real regarding our place on this earth. We are literally just babies from the biological sense of the universe, there is no denying this. All I have to do is look to a sea turtle, or the ginkgo tree and see them for what they are – millions of years of experience on this earth. Sorry to disappoint all my friends and colleagues in biology, sciences, physics, and psychology, but, we still essentially know very little in comparison to our "elder" earth inhabitants. We have much to learn. Just because they do not use our word-based language, does not make them less intelligent, in fact, the lack of the need to place labels to make sense of things makes their capacity to be aware much more in tune. Think about it; what happens to a person who loses their sight? All of their other senses are heightened, especially their "spatial sense" and "feeling energy senses." There has been studies for years that beyond wildlife (bees, etc.) that people who cannot see can sense fear, or other feeling energies transmitted from others around them. They are more aware than some of us when we are tense.

We are like toddlers according to the universe. Isn't that a neat way to help level the playing field when we do come across a leader or expert? No matter what research they present, or proposals and knowledge they

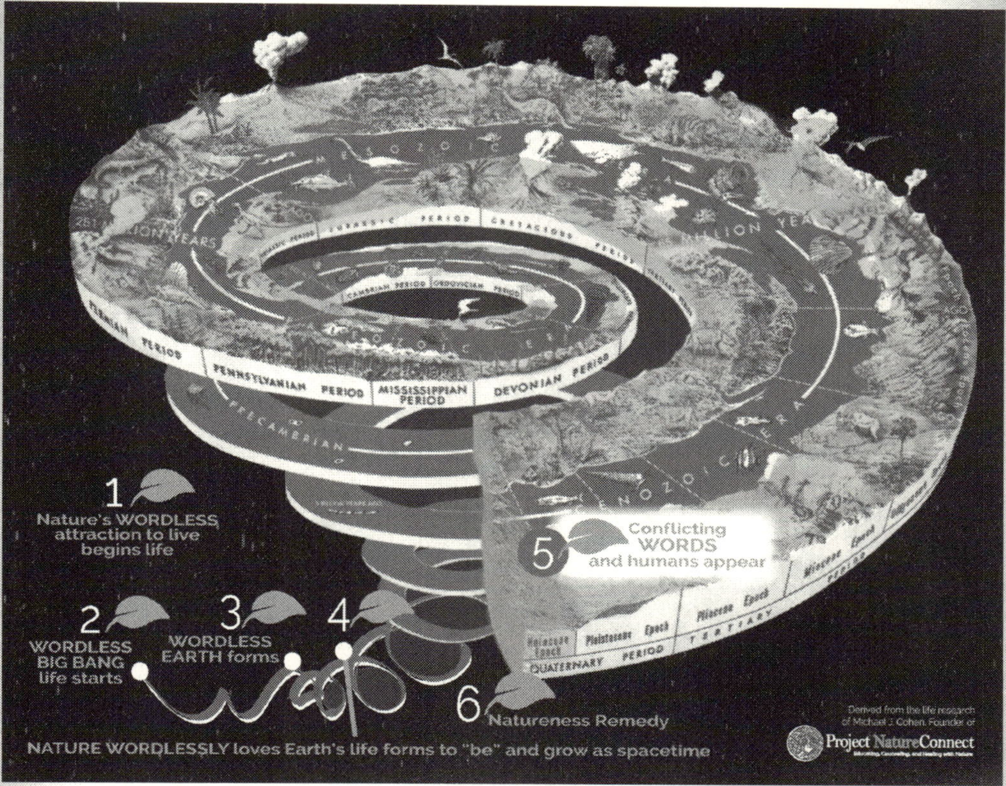

share, it still does not take away the fact that all humans are still toddlers in this universe. Whew. I don't know about you, but once I realized this, I felt so much better about my place in our society's established "hierarchy." The largest thing I learned upon this realization is that, I can still respect all the research gathered, and respect an individual's devotion and hard work, but I am free to make up my own mind and present any human revelation, idea or development to nature – tapping into that consciousness either by visiting my favorite sea turtle or looking up at the 150 year old Pony Tail Palm tree in my back yard.

Above is just glimpse into how "young' we are, and how much we do not know when it comes the forces of life. This is an illustration I collaborated with Dr. Michael Cohen, (founder of ProjectNature Connect). We derived it

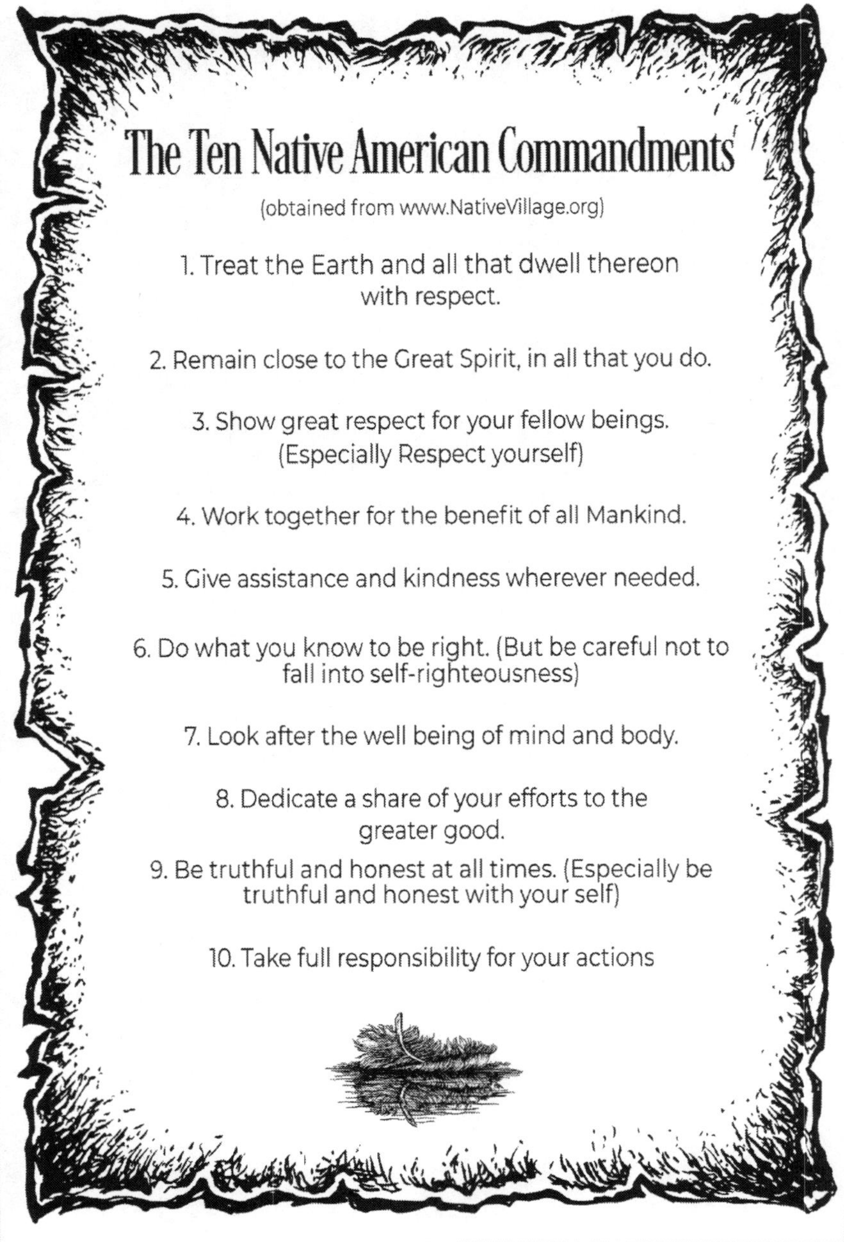

The Ten Native American Commandments

(obtained from www.NativeVillage.org)

1. Treat the Earth and all that dwell thereon with respect.

2. Remain close to the Great Spirit, in all that you do.

3. Show great respect for your fellow beings. (Especially Respect yourself)

4. Work together for the benefit of all Mankind.

5. Give assistance and kindness wherever needed.

6. Do what you know to be right. (But be careful not to fall into self-righteousness)

7. Look after the well being of mind and body.

8. Dedicate a share of your efforts to the greater good.

9. Be truthful and honest at all times. (Especially be truthful and honest with your self)

10. Take full responsibility for your actions

from an image which has been circling the science world for decades. Living a healthy island life at the age of 96, Mike continues to write about our disconnect with nature. His approach is different, which is why it is not widely

Colonial Ten Commandments

(obtained from King James Version Bible)

1 You shall have no other gods before me.

2 You shall not make for yourself any carved image, or any likeness of anything that is in heaven above, or that is in the earth beneath, or that is in the water under the earth; you shall not bow down to them nor serve them.

3 You shall not take the name of the Lord your God in vain, for the Lord will not hold him guiltless who takes His name in vain.

4 Remember the Sabbath day, to keep it holy.

5 Honor your father and your mother, that your days may be long upon the land which the Lord your God is giving you.

6 You shall not murder.

7 You shall not commit adultery.

8 You shall not steal.

9 You shall not bear false witness against your neighbor.

10 You shall not covet your neighbor's house; you shall not covet your neighbor's wife, nor his manservant, nor his maidservant, nor his ox, nor his donkey, nor anything that is your neighbor's."

acknowledged. He accepts this purely because he stays primarily in the "wordlessness" of nature. I appreciate all his books and approach because he is pointing out the truth. We need to balance our minds with the sensory intelligence from ancient wordless sources if we are ever going to mature as a species on a planet that has been intelligently operating just fine without us.

We are still struggling to find the path that works. I know this struggle merely from our constant disagreements on religion and politics. Back to that Titanic statement: the arguing about human stories that are no longer serving us is just like arguing about where to place the furniture on a sinking ship. Yet, we must be fully aware that it is the "humanity" ride that is at risk, because Earth is just going to keep being Earth. We are not here to "save Earth." My brand marketer mind has always questioned why the envrionmental messaging continues to fall flat, and I know have come to the conclusion that we must stop blaming the "big guys" in power, because the power is in numbers now. And it is the responsiblity of adapting communications which fully land in the minds and hearts of many cultures - purely in the shared interest of our common ground and kinship.

I am doing everything to avoid in-depth conversation on both of these topics, by the way. This book is about us a individuals and our relationship with ourselves and nature. My view is we are all in this together because we all need the air to breathe, the water to drink, and the soil and sun. At the end of the day, we all have to eat, drink, go to the bathroom, love, laugh and cry. So, back to my proof of why are still babies figuring things out. I searched and compared several "commandments" floating around out there, striving to find the common ground. (Well, our common ground is the earth's ground, but some folks seem to have forgotten that...whatever, I'm so not going there today).

We didn't know what we didn't know

Rules or "Guidelines?" Now, for comparison sake only with regard to our human-language dominated world of today, and not to start a religious debate whatsoever is a few examples of "rules" we have set for ourselves. I have a Catholic and Christian background, and I still hold dear the values that I was taught with some respects, however, I have simply found that it is ok to read and consider many other approaches and respect others, yet knowing when to apply the "take what you like and leave the rest approach" in my years 12 step recovery world. We all have the right to choose what works for us individually. My main point in sharing these is that we can embrace how humanity really strives to morality, and the commonalities of these rules – or, guidelines for life. Then, we can make decisions out in nature by looking from all of them from our life source and see what works for us in our journey to self-care and fully participating in the web of life.

Expanding our lens to new mindsets

These are just two just to expand our minds to the fact that different cultures are going to have different lenses of the world. I spend many years learning the abundance of variations from different cultures.

After many years of my own deconstructing of what "truth" is, combined with my past decade of restoring my kinship with the natural world, for me the Native American 10 Commandments seem to be the most aligned with my values. Why? Because it is of a more collaborative, nature-centered mindset, and honestly less authoritative than the others. This list is the most harmonious with nature and our natural selves.

I am here to merely share my journey, yet I do strongly recommend a deep dive into the history of humanity. The limited lens from my own American education, and my identity as one who checks the word "caucasion" in the boxes on forms throughout this country, it was quite the liiberating and enlightening experience.

After much studying, and years of deconstructing which is a story anchored in reality, and which is not, I did choose to claim my pedestrian status - a pedstrian walking the Earth, which happens to be the creating source of all that is needed for humans to exist. Having said that, I understand how hard it is to unpack what was stated as truth for so long, and punishment and shame for even questioning anything - so I undertand and respect anyone who chooses to stay where they are comfortable.

I choose to go with a "real" tangible God I understand, and have immediate access to, and who also communicates back - which is why I created the acronym:

Great Ominipotent Driver (of Life Force)

It's greater than we are
It knows more that we do
And it's driving, not us.

As a Catholic High School graduate, I felt just fine with this because the other God after many walks in nature, told me it was just fine. The main thought that I kept hearing in my mind was, "as long as you walk the Earth with reverence and respect of all of life, you're good. Certain groups have warped my brand anyway for their own gains, so go at it."

We weren't taught this

When we are in the midst of a specific culture, our lens is taught in that culture's ways. So after my initial anger I felt about facts of history, other lenses being introduced, my mind bvegan to ease as I simply began the discovery adventure of the abundance of options. It isn't our fault if we were conditioned within a specific culture as children, with stories that are limited to a specific mindset. And the good news is, we can embark upon the journey of discovery of all lenses. I found it is so much easier to acknowledge what works, and what doesn't work when grounded in the driving force of life, nature. It helps ground the mind in the common ground of humanity.

Giving ourselves permission

Now if ther has been some discomfort from this discussion so far, then that is purely from the stories that have been so deeply implanted inside the mind. Our brains are like computers (since computers are a human creation, they do mirror us), and we only operate from what software is loaded in. There cannot be a shift until that thought process if disrupted, with new information and stories.

Beginning our story discernment trail

Every time I connect with nature, I so feel the excitement, and the freedom to give myself permission to explore, discover and discern.

This is where the Lighten Up Trail Map can be used as a guide to discover what is weighing us down, and what is lightening us up. Yet, adding into this the "whys." The "whys" as in are they healthy, do they align with our natural selves, or are the feel good parts, or hanging onto the no-so-good parts part of an old story we having been looping around? Nature is that unbiased lens from which to look through, it is a mirror to us.

This is also where the Mind-Heart Trail Map can really help. When we continously ask ourselves what our mind says, our heart says, and then incorporate what nature says, we become so much closer to the answers we seek about our natural selves, and what we truly desire.

Note: I have found ending out gratitude signals (good vibe energy) when interacting with nature really increases the amount of energy that comes back from Nature without fail. Simple math, the more in need of comfort, wisdom and guidance...the more gratitude signals sent, I will receive back what is needed. Plus, most natural beings out there are used to "unplugged," "un-sensory aware" humans, so they definitely notice the difference in the vibe. And remembering that the old stories tell you nature is out to hurt you, or is dangerous, dirty... it's quite simple. Most natural beings just want to go along in their life and honestly just want the same respect we expect.

Understanding your relationship with nature, is an epic journey in understanding yourself, with others.

Take baby steps! One step at a time.

Gingko Hug ~ P. Hoke

Gingko is the oldest living tree, and has the capacity to regenerate itself forever, if not externally affected. I I I love this genius tree species because of its beautiful smooth leaf designs, yet also because of its healing powers for human minds.

CHAPTER 6

Our Brains on Nature and Art

We can learn how to live life, by simply observing and taking notes from the source of life, nature.

Research is increasingly showing heightened brain activity and decreasing stress levels when a human goes to nature. This is something that can be looked up all over the Internet. The key is seizing this on a habitual basis. What I introduce is taking in mental notes of nature as if it is a new prescription that the doctor put on your pill bottle. Your self-written prescription with the only side effects being you feel more intelligent, confident and peaceful. I say this because others around you may not understand it, and most likely will react to your growing lack of reactions to them staying int the mental collective crazies. This is your own personal, unique journey, and no one can take this medicine away from you. There is actually no such thing as over-dosing on nature, with perhaps the exception of those who may take it over the top and not balance with responsibilities that still exist in our human-made world. Our human-made society is still nature, because we are nature, so yes, we still participate and embrace that part of us, too – but Knowing and acknowledging the natural world on a daily, hourly, weekly basis...whatever can be worked into a daily life that makes sense in both worlds is the secret to a happier path. We create our "nature reward time," and slowly feel this reward, this personal pleasure, just like we would a cup of coffee, a glass of wine, a cigarette, a piece of chocolate cake, or shopping trip for a new item. We can gradually add this mental escape to our thought process because we know it is only going to make us feel good, feel more intelligent, more peaceful, and more aware. Just like that research shows, the coritsol levels go down, and the endorphins go up!

Here are the facts we need to reckon with. Mostly to drill into our minds that the current situation of humanity now requires we adapt to our technological age (where computers are doing most of the linear left-brain thinking), we get to be freed up to embrace all those other hidden competencies and talents. Simple do an online search of these phrases, and you will see what I mean. There are endless You Tube videos also (it's ok, we do have a form of attention deficit, and we can embrace that in a way that works for us now to become layered with a tapestry of skills and talents!)

The Conceptual Age - Creative Age
Durable Skills - New Economy - Circular Economy - Adaptive Leadership - Adaptive Intelligence - Social Intelligence - Emotional Intelligence - Creative Intelligence - Our Brains on Nature - Our Brains on Art

The research is clear, we will not survive, even as individuals unless we expand into using these natural capacities and skillsets. And the good news is, we can re-ignite all of them, yet, it requires us to retrain our brains. We can do this by the awareness check with a simple "pause." The pause, reflect, respond method is what has been working for me for well over a decade now, for a multitude of ways I have been retraining my brain so I can adapt. It disrupts the old story loop and shows my brain I mean business!

I have to share something special with that thought. Just last week, Angela told me she wished we could spend some time in a culture where we did not know the language at all, and just "feel and love the people for who they are." My heart leaped with joyful burst, feeling so privileged to hear such wise words! She later expressed after the activity that she felt very much comfort and love for just "being" and knowing a peaceful language at the pond when we were sitting with our feet in the pond, feeling the smooth algae touch our feet on the ledge underneath, enjoying the lizard, and the goldfish life. She and I both agreed that by not speaking, closing our eyes, we can better know that world which we want to know better and bond with it, to feel fully connected to it long enough to receive it's sensory communication, it's information that is not numbers or words.

"I found I could say things with color and shapes that I couldn't say any other way — things I had no words for."
- Georgia O'Keefe

Our Brain Structure according to neuroscientists for decades

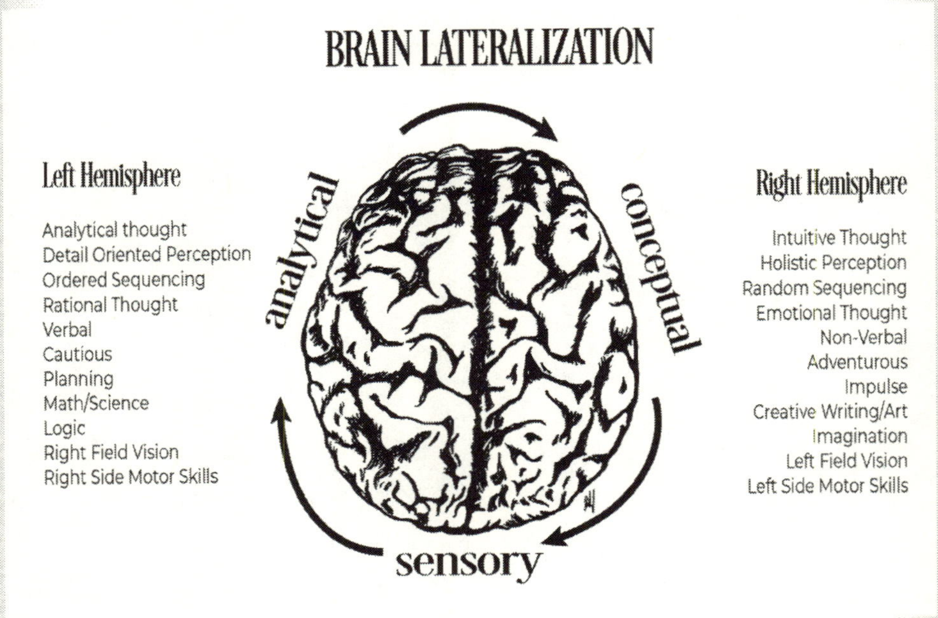

There has never been any argument about which side does what. The issue is the dominant, controlling might I add, mindset that has hijacked our modern societies that keeps us in that scarcity mind, that fear of ambiguity, and so many other fears. See the left side part about "cautious?" We need to rationally learn to assess which situations are truly dangerous that need our flight or flight mode, yes. However, our brains, therefore our bodies work in harmony to create scenarios of fear when there is only something "new" or different.

When I allow myself to really "feel" life – being still to hear and see what life is saying to me in nature, I feel more complete as a human. It is only by learning how to shut off the verbal language and the societal habit of over-thinking things in reason, which gives me wisdom and comfort within a world language that I long lost yet very much needed. I found that I can do this in the most healthiest of techniques - with nature and art.

A fun activity to help the connecting with nature process

Go out to your nature space or natural attraction of the moment with your nature journal. Make a list of your wants, needs and desires. Make another list of what you are willing to do in nature. For example, some of us have been told not to go barefoot – the fear was instilled early on - but maybe we would like to try. Maybe we just never realized the value of it, or considered the sensations we are missing out on when we keep our shoes on. We can trust in our natural senses (common senses) to tell us when it is safe to do so.
Now, start a plan on addressing each of #2, with #3. Look to the first natural attractions and studying them for a while. Try to see any parts that you identify with – such as how a fly is attracted to certain things, the bee is pulled toward certain colors, or why a leaf turns a certain way. Maybe the wind is strong, it is raining, or it is very sunny outside – try to pull these happenings in nature into your psyche as messages, relate them to your moments by scribbling around your list some of the swirls, or basic raindrop shapes, or streaming sunshine rays. Circle the most exciting parts of your list and try to identify with what is around you – make analogies. Making a habit of creating analogies with what you sense in nature, is a practice of making mental, sensory connections with your

natural surroundings - animals, insects, even clouds can bring you into thinking like and with nature, placing you into your natural state. This is how you can sense things and think more clearly, making you more intelligent and creative – therefore deriving more intelligent and creative decisions. Try doing these analogies anywhere, even on the work commute, just looking out the window, or just feeling the life in the produce in the grocery store.

The more you try to create mental escapes with nature wherever you are, and more often you do it, the better you will feel and find yourself wanting to do it more often. Each natural experience when fully into it mentally, will help you to be better equipped to handle just about any situation presented to you. You also begin to learn how to grab quick insight into what you already know and feel within just by following your individual natural attractions and identifying with them. Once you validate them in your safe nature space in your mind, no one can take them away.

What begins to happen that is most important, is you really do begin to trust in the sensations and signals from nature, because you begin to identify yourself as very much a part of them – not separate. You can begin to sense that feeling that you are happening with nature, because you are very much part of nature as a natural being. With knowing nature is the tangible part right of front of you that you can reach out to at any given moment, you allow yourself to communicate mentally with it – you are officially "plugged into" it's wisdom, and it's good feelings. You will begin to realize that you never want that taken away, and begin to cherish each experience. Nature begins to be your guide and remind you of what you know and feel at all times is valid, it is, reality – your reality. This allows you to begin to make room to balance natural self with the new brain world of language and civilization.

So begin your nature dosage plan, your art-dosage plan to retrain your mind. Try to write out or sketch your nature and art wish list, and look forward to the intelligence, creativity and clarity you get to receive while having fun. Then, don't wait around, get to the simplest ones right away, even if it is simply taking 5 minutes to enjoy and sense that bird that keeps showing up near your office window, or stopping to just touch that beautiful tree you pass by each day, and begin sensing why you are attracted to it. It is a win-win! If you would like, try this "whole mind" map to map out your abilities, and see what comes up (using the circle technique from the last chapter).

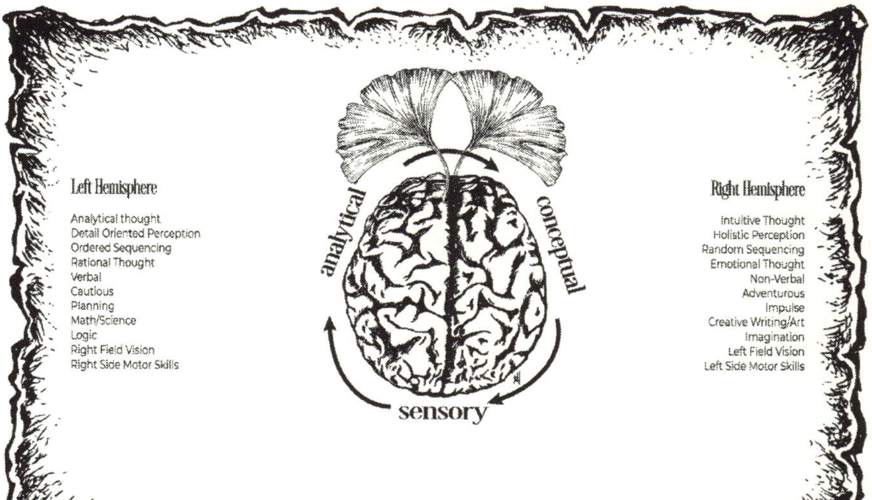

A Whole Human Mind Map | Natural Self Discovery, copyright 2024

Ollie's Eyes ~ P. Hoke

Ollie was a dear friend from Treasure Coast Wildlife Center in Florida, a rescued educational Barred Owl, with limited eyesight. He helped myself and my art students bond with and paint from his lens.

CHAPTER 7

Seeing the Forest Like the Trees

Here is the most important tool of this journey, to create a habit, a practice viewing our world from nature's lens.

Trees have a better sense of community

There are dozens of books that literally have the title "wisdom of trees" included. There are so many because the truth is out There is actual, scientific evidence that trees work together to sustain their community. From their intricate network of roots and communication systems of fungi which mirror our computer systems (and the dynamics of our brains), to the collective warning they can send each other through chemical releases above the ground.

My favorite of the books that I have read about trees so far has to be "The Hidden Life of Trees," by Peter Wohlleben. The subtitle essentially says it all, "...what they feel, how they communicate - discoveries from a secret world." And this world shows clearly how trees "love" each other, and "love" life. What is so amazing about this particular book about trees is Peter is a former arborist, in that his job was to decide which trees were logged or not. He shares his incredible journey of how he begins to sense this amazing life as he was immersed in it. I cannot come up with a better way to share with you how to being to see the forest "like" the trees.

We always have that saying, "see the forest through the trees," which shows yet again how our dominant linear thinking has omitted our kinship mindset with nature. We can see how being completely immersed in being raised in this mindset has limited our capacity to fully grasp that we can have an intimate relationship with all of nature. And this does mean a balanced one, where we live in our human world and the realities which that entails, yet gradually brining in the "wisdom of trees" into our thinking and into how we navigate life as ultimate teachers.

Learn flexibility from trees

A first lesson about trees when it comes to us learning to ditch the fear stories that are actually harming us, is that they are flexible. Their branches are all designed to go with most winds, and most trees, when they are in their natural environment that is, have root systems designed to withstand weather events. Let's zoom out and think about how we could be more flexible, more adapted to our environments? Since weather patterns are changing, and we do have the luxury (unlike a tree community), to plan to move to a location that make more sense depending on our situation.

Trees teach us how to let go

We always look forward to autumn simply from the colors, and perhaps crisper air. I have always looked forward to it because I do love the scent of decaying leaves, especially playing in them by my huge oak tree friend in my childhood back yard. The scent of change, which in life does mean something has to die to sustain - cells have to die. It took me until I had breast cancer to accept this part of our biology, and how cancer cells are cells masking themselves as normal cells, yet do not participate in the cycle necessary to sustain life by refusing to die. The amazing thing is, after the full cycle of radiation where cells where killed to kill those pesky cells, I felt a huge sense of newness after 7 years - why? Because our entire body is composed of entirely new cells every 7 years!

This brings me to autumn and letting go. Mel Robbins, one of my absolute favorite authors and podcast host, has a wonderful story about autumn leave and how trees show us to let go. The trees know they are about to hit winter, with scarce access to sunlight for the leaves, and scarce water. The only way the tree will survive the winter is to shed those leaves because it will not have the resources to feed the leaves. If we were to do a full map of this dynamic in relation to a current situation in life that is weighing us down, we might just arrive at some sensible, sustainable and yes, loving conclusions. I have learned the hard way throughout my life challenges that sometime letting go of someone is the most loving things we can do for them, ourselves and the whole of the life experience.

Now that we have unpacked the validity of the fact we are nature, once we truly allow that to "land" in mind and body, practice this mindset, create analogies, metaphors, envision "what would nature do," we've got this. As we deepen this understanding that nature is a mirror to us, and we are a mirror to it, then we have a chance of creating a healthier relationship with our life source. We also then create healthier relationships with ourselves and each others.

Aligning our thinking with the natural world

By learning to now enter a wooded area in this lens, it becomes easier and easier to take our natural world experiences to a whole new level of depth, insight, and new intelligence. If we can go without distractions, meaning yes, without dogs that will deter the full experiences and encounters with curious natural beings, and without our earbuds on so we can experience all of the area while increasing our natural sensory awarenesses. We truly can begin to restore all those hidden right-brain capacities, along with all the proven physiological and mental benefits.

We can continue by creating serious trail maps and strategies as a priority to help us see the forest like the trees, the birds, the owls, and all of the community that works together, in harmony to sustain life. We learn to align our thought processes with the genius of these ecosystems and all of their inhabitants. This is especially useful if those areas are near your home - because then you "know" that natural area very well because you have a relationship with it. And if there are resources there that might be needed in an emergency (edible plants, water that could be filtered, etc.), as kin with that area, you will have access to it and understand the symbiotic part of it.

So moving forward, this chapter was all about introducing this concept of seeing like nature, yet also thinking like AND WITH nature. Also feeling like, and with nature because the more we are in community with it, we do feel that sense of belonging, and a deep sense of purpose in our restored relationship with it - just as we would if we were to enter into a relationship with our fellow humans. Yet, this natural world relationship is void of the old stories which are causing harm, and is all about the language of "love," of intimacy, of sensory awareness communication that is not filtered with words. We get to achieve that depth in our life experience which we crave. We get to answer that deep yearning for access to nature simply by opening up to this new lens.

Here are few other tips to help you on this mindset and begin to process how this changes your worldview and your relationship with yourself, yet also how this process impacts how you show up in relationships with your family, loved ones, friends, and can even inform new strategies for your career relationships and working with purpose in with your natural talents and strengths.

Learn habitual association and identification with natural areas and beings you are attracted to.

Create Nature Metaphors that you can carry with you as guides in situations

Create natural experiences, nature moments as part of your day,

Take lots of nature notes! Including doodles/sketches (to learn to merge your word mind with sensory mind - hybrid thinking patterns)

We can begin to sense a natural area, natural being, and a natural object's form in our minds because simply because it is near and we feel it – without labels/words. From my personal experiences in these states of mind, I now realize I feel an increased awareness of the natural mental senses of relaxation which help me achieve a meditative state much easier both! Courage to see the forest like the trees and feeling all my senses

A lot of my courage to adapt and embrace change was probably rooted in my most challenging life experiences, and the fact that I had the privilege of becoming accustomed to being that misfit – always pushing the envelope, always ruffling feathers. I have to thank my grandfather and my mother and father for those traits.

The most recent lesson that helped me truly grasp every ounce of courage to be open to diving into feeling all my senses, and begin trusting in the life shifts I wanted to make to keep the momentum of good feelings I received from this process, had to be I recalled my son's time in boot camp. This inspired me to begin the move back to our old house with just my daughter. (Tim was back in rehab at the time and it was another tough love situation for our relationship). I felt Alex's pain of that training and with each box loaded and unloaded, I thought of every sit up and push up he had to face. If he could do that, I could make it through this. Now nearly two years later, I thought of his Airborne training, mixed up with the oddities of the Presidential election and the horrific events above, and said to myself, "alright , if my son can leap from an airplane and be willing to prepare himself for deployment, surely I can write a f**king book."

Yes, I swear when it is important, my love for our language is how we have created these expressive words that actually do relieve. John Parkin validates this smoothly and humorously enough for even the tightest of rigid minds to let loose in his book, F**k It. (Yes, at this point, I feel comfortable spelling it out, and hopefully those of you offended by the word have perhaps chilled out a bit). His book also helped me through this deadline thing for my book. I said "f**k it," write the book and trust that whoever is attracted to reading it will...or not.

The most important step, however, is just learning to be good to yourself...self care, self love is NOT selfish like the old stories shamed us into- it is sensible - it is for sustainability: the meaning of life, to "sustain" life. That self-care and self-love can be fully discovered with experiencing all of your natural senses and innate intelligences. This is essentially the core ingredient to plugging into the planet, therefore, plugging back into your natural self.

It is all about ditching the old that is not working and letting in the new "known" that works

To retrain our minds to "see" like nature, to think like nature, and feel like nature, we simply have to create the habit to be with it, and mentally connect with it. Either through creating metaphors, associations, and especially by identification - yet I am speaking of taking us a step far beyond just environmental education. Creating moments that create true kinship, not just the left brain linear knowledge without substance, without depth and meaning.

This is a new way to approach in creating a deep, sensory, intimate relationship with nature as kin, yet applies to how to navigate life in general. That means with people, yet really try to take it a step further, and consider how you make nature feel when you are in proximity to it.

Does the natural being or area feel threatened, or relaxed? As we move more into an intimate relationship (which is, as a reminder,part of our primary human needs discussed earlier), we experience a fulfillment just in the gift of getting to have an experience with whatever being, and however they consent to. To be a respectful natural being connecting with the natural world, it does require respect, a mutual, consensual, symbiotic relationship (back to simple cells of how life operates).

That is enough to contemplate for now. Beyond the quote below, I have some activities to help encourage this particular shift toward your natural mind - your "whole human mind."

Here is a way to begin to contemplate, reflect on how nature mirrors to us what we are seeking, if only we pause and look. This map is also referenced later on in our strategic response phase. Yet I wanted to introduce it here as an example of metaphor building, and creating associations and learning from the intelligence of the natural world. We need to constantly remind ourselves, it is the expert on how to do "life." A cyclical, regenerative, sensible and actually "loving" way to do life in harmony with others. This Alignment Strategy Map can help you individually, yet also applies to organizational planning and team building. It is mostly to assist in the awareness of a tree stump - yes feel the grief in that - yet learn from the growth process of a tree from it, and see how it does inspire us to look outside ourselves and see ourselves in nature's community, so we are stronger for our human community.

An Activity to go even deeper if you dare

Plug into all of your senses so you can really begin seeing the forest like the trees! Grab your nature journal and head to the natural attraction that calls to you.

Pick 1 or more of the senses from the list, and relate them to the natural attraction, either through analogies, similarities from the obvious senses – color, texture, ambiance, etc. What feelings or awareness's arise? You could reverse the process by going to the natural attraction and let it guide to which of the senses on the list you feel at the time. If possible, over time, try to go through each of the senses, and discover which ones are strongest within you, which ones you completely took for granted, which ones help you feel more aware and alive once re-connected on a deeper conscious level.

With time and practice of awareness of each of these senses, you naturally begin to sense that overall connection to nature and are communicating with it without even realizing it…it becomes, well, your 1st nature. As our modern "literate" society puts it…they become our 2nd nature, but it is essentially our first and foremost as we are nature! Once these realizations become truth, each time they become stronger and more intense as your conscious begins to really absorb the information and feelings exchanged with nature. Congratulations, you

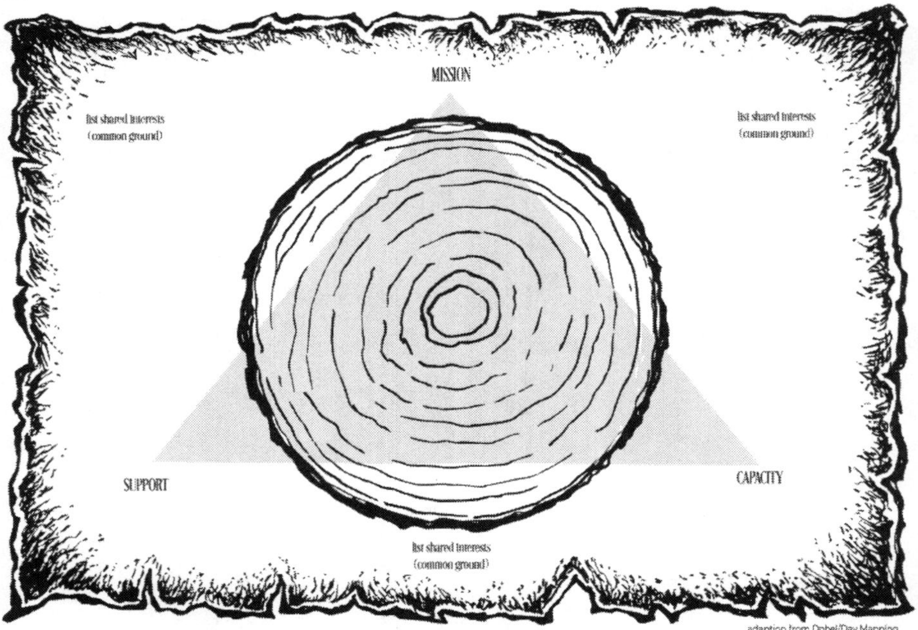

Natural Alignment Strategy Map | Natural Self Discovery, copyright 2024

adaption from Dobel/Day Mapping

have tapped back into that genius, you are officially communicating with nature – you are nature literate and no one can take that away from you. You will begin to trust each of your senses more and more every time you acknowledge them and make room for them into your consciousness. It helps to notate or doodle the attractions that helped you along in this heightened awareness. It really does begin to feel as if you are plugging into a higher source of information and good feelings beyond what any traditional meditation from within can provide. Each of the senses becomes enhanced and stronger, the intelligences become just that, and you will find yourself more aware and feeling than ever before.

Enjoy and celebrate each new revelation, as each one brings you closer to your natural self and all the creative intelligences and awareness's you have had all along!

Tender Turt, Rescued Green Sea Turtle ~ P. Hoke

Turt was in bad shape from a boating accident when I first met him at Loggerhead Marinline Center. I got to be a part of his recovery journey, his injuries prevented him from being released, yet he now has a forefer home at Florida Oceanographic Coastl Center. He inspired me to learn a new painting medium.

CHAPTER 8

Making Sense of the Senseless

"We can move toward acceptance then take ourselves through a natural path of grieving then letting go."

First, let's just make this clear, we are all senseless right now, some more than others, purely from our disconnection from the natural world.

Now, having said that, let's envision what our version of a trail map of the senselessness of how our fellow humans are behaving and thinking would look like. And, that is what I would suggest the first exercise be around this topic. Either using the trail map, tree map, or other natural symbol you created in your mind that helps you connect it all. I found it so helpful and fun to play with humans shapes in that trail. However, it also helped grieve that atrocious behaviors and what other humans and natural world beings are experiencing at the cost some very hurt humans that have become trapped and warped by nature-disconnected stories and hurts by others.

Hurt People Hurt People

This is a saying that I learned, and held close during this last decade in my support groups. It has helped me in making sense of the senselessness of the situation of humanity, our communities, our economy, etc, - yet also the senseless state of many humans. The numbness. The apathy. Some who have shoved down so much purely from the dominant linear thinking systems of modern humanity. After much of this journaling work (I have journaled most of my life - that is a whole other book as to why yet mostly to keep my mind effectively balanced in my multiple careers), I am finally able to step back and grasp this reality about people who exhibit awful behavior.

One of my recent favorite books from my graduate school chrysalis period this past two years, was Non-Violent Communication, by Rosenberg. It was written back in , yet what he introduced was some incredibly profound techniques to de-escalate even the most terrifying encounters with hurt humans. And the main point is pausing just briefly, enough to process the energy of that moment and the energy coming from the human that is struggling. With increased sensory awareness skills, we can actually "sense" the hurt in the person. And when we get down to it, back to human needs: our need to be acknowledged - or "seen" and heard."

I also recommend Alexis Carter's "Ask for More" - 10 Questions" This book was part of a strategic negotiations course, and was by far the most profound and effective research in how to negotiate with our fellow humans, especially when they are hurt by something. The main things is listening. Active listening and open questions, and "tell me more." The techniques in this book, and the entire course have helped me navigate some very confusing relationship situations, yet have also helped me make sense of some the awful things I feel so angered by when it comes to how humans treat nature. Also, I can find myself get angry with the continued harm our current systems cause to children by denying them access to the arts and a relationship with nature, so they can use their whole minds. My grief also goes to all of us adults who now get to restore these two core missing parts of our human experience.

By learning to accept that somewhere a person was hurt, and is merely in a bodily reaction from that hurt, I have been able to even grasp what goes through the minds of trophy hunters, for example. I know that is heavy, yet it weighs heavy on my heart and mind. I have concluded that they are hurt by their separation from nature, and without knowing it, their inner yearning for a connection with has been warped by the dominant mindset that does promote violence - I sense that what they are seeking, without being conscious of it, is a connection with the animal. What if we could simply shift that horrible practice into excursions where this need to have a connection with an animal is what is yearned for? What if we could being mapping out the root of why people are so neglectful and abusive to their pets and wildlife? They were obviously denied the opportunity to create a an authentic kinship with the natural world. This perhaps could demonstrate how it ended up that hurt people now hurt people? Or, that so many people have been harmed by the dominant linear, left-side thinking from their upbringing, that it now spills out onto others. Yes. All This. My point is, once we can feel something, fine a path to empathize for those we are so angry at, we can actually get to making sense of the senselessness of humans.

"Sensory Intelligence"

The most important thing we can do is become more sensory aware, acknowledging and fully using all of our bodily senses. Think of the caterpillar again. It "senses" it's way to it's food source, it "senses" it's way to a safe place where it will build its cocoon while it transforms. Our senses are ignited by stimuli around us, and from what science is showing, there still is not full agreement on how many we truly have. I am still looking, and have been for a while. Recently on Scientific American, it was finally acknowledged that we do have more senses beyond the "five" that our dominant linear thinking delivered to us for centuries. That we do have expanded senses that yes, use all of the others, or in combination, yet, there is still those "feelings" we get, like picking up on energy vibrations from another person or natural being. This goes far beyond the smelling of pheromone releases for example, or far beyond our ability to "sense" with foresight. It goes beyond our ability to project thought and predict future events from what has already happened, or with data. So the consensus is there is no "consensus," except there is that "something else" sense as they call the 6th sense - yet being a realist, and desire to seek tactile truth with nature, I listed below a combination of the phrases we use every day in describing "senses," with the hierarchy of human needs, and added in the ones that I myself have experienced from doing nature connecting exercises that were developed by a mix of many variations of human senses out there. My "sense" is that all of us get to validate what we sense, and most importantly beginning to value how amazingly intelligent our bodies are in that they are always functioning to sustain our life! And, we can process so much information, and we can appreciate how our bodies are so connected to the natural world just from sensing gravity. We can also celebrate that simply by becoming more and more in tune with these as a form of intelligence, :intuition," we will have an increased ability to navigate any situation, and discern when our bodies are signaling something that we need addresses (health, surroundings, etc.)

So here is a list of sense for us to start "sensing" life fully, and becoming more sensory aware.

Vision, Hearing (sensing vibrations also), Touch, Taste Smell - Sense of unity, community - Sense of belonging - Sense of self - Sense of proximity, space - Sense of others - Aesthetic Sense, Color Sense
Sense of hunger, thirst, elimination
Sense of the seasons/winter hibernation/sleep - spring active - Sense of gravity/pressure -wind, air, ground - Sense of movement
Sense of direction, land and sea - navigation
Sense of polarity and electromagnetic charges
Sense of temperature, humidity
Hormonal sense, as to pheromones and other chemical stimuli (by other natural beings also) - Procreative urges - Territorial sense, prey. Psychic sense - foreknowledge, clairvoyance, clairaudience

What got my attention - the Gulf Oil Spill

Go with the flow - and, in this case, go with the flow of the devastation of oil in our precious Gulf - which essentially in my mind spells the need for change by us all.

My change? I woke up staring at "Turtwig," a Green Sea Turtle patient at Loggerhead Marinelife Center in Juno Beach, FL, my next celebrity to be on canvas. As the morning light hit the sketch on my patio, I glanced at the oil paints and it hit me right in the gut...that does not make sense anymore. I realize that obviously crude oil is not the same as the linseed oils in the paints...it's the principle, and psychological effect from the thought of visualizing all the creatures that will soon be covered in oil. This thought, coupled with the solvents that come with using oil paints have simply led me to make this as a moral decision that was long overdue. If I am going to strive to help, I too, must change - however I can. So, today - out with the oil paints and the harmful chemicals that come with them, and in with acrylics...with just water. It's a start. I haven't painted in acrylics for a while...but the investment now in supplies and time is priceless to me, and it's just simply a moral responsibility in my mind now. (I can't believe I didn't switch sooner...I use watercolors a lot, well better now than never.)

Carl Safina posted an incredible perspective on the catastrophic oil spill, "Spill Baby Spill"...it really baked my noodle, that's for sure. Thank you, Carl, for being a voice of reason. You are not shoving radical concepts down people's throats, and you are not sitting idly by as the toxic oil threatens to shove itself down the throats of precious wildlife that are the most intricate part of the ecosystem that keeps our oceans thriving.

What this spill should do for our country is spell C-H-A-N-G-E... But, not change that mandates what people do (can't step on freedom, just make bad things un-cool, like we have with smoking), and definitely not change that will cause major economic damage, nor change that provides a constant hand-out to those who do not wish to earn what they have - yet what a about a change of mindset, just a change in our attitudes that one step is at least a start? How can we begin to at least TRY to be more responsible and preserve earth for our families and our grandchildren's' future? Open our minds to go with the flow... adapt like nature has to adapt? (Note: Earth does not belong to US, we get the privilege being here to enjoy it, not destroy it.) We need to begin the conversation for change - and the necessary message that Sylvia Earle has been striving to drive home for years, that our Oceans are the foundation of life here on earth. You can learn more about Sylvia and this vital message that we need to drive home either through her talk on TED posted at Mission-Blue.org, or by grabbing her book "The World is Blue: How Our Fate and the Ocean's Are One." The World Is Blue: How Our Fate and the Ocean's Are One.

What can each of us do that is a REALISTIC step? Even if it's just ONE behavior, at least it 's SOMETHING, it's a start

"The journey of a thousand miles begins with one small step."

-Lao Tzu

I was so grateful to be consoled by, and continued guidance to help me personally make sense of the senseless tragedy of the Gulf Oil spill by Carl Safina, renowned biologists, marine conservationist and author. In his book Sea of Flames he begins to make sense of it all in his conscious, referring to the first responders, and who did and didn't do what, he says so well, "But it's not all about them. It's about us. We all contributed to this event and we're all trapped in the same situation. We all use too much gasoline and oil, because we've painted ourselves into a corner when it comes to energy."

What I so appreciate about this is how Carl moves us beyond the intricacies and finger-pointing of the ones on top who were essentially responsible, and pulls everyone in. I felt engaged enough, but that's just me. I always try to look beyond the negativity, as I realize so many just couldn't watch anymore, nor look at photos or read about the horrific reality. Well, it is reality, and the reality does lie with all of us together. But, to me, this is the great news. There is something we can do, as I faced it, and did a part I could. This is healing, my friends. But the initial pain has to be experienced for one to grow. Admitting the problem is the first step toward recovery. The longer we keep the blinders on, the longer we stay sick. So, we can let the healing begin.

As stated so well by Dr. Safina, "The worst environmental disaster in history isn't the oil that got away. The real catastrophe is the oil we don't spill. It's the oil we run through our engines as intended. It's the oil we burn, the coal we burn, the gas we burn. The worst spill—the real catastrophe—is the carbon dioxide we spill out of our tailpipes and smokestacks every second of every day, year upon decade. That spill is changing the atmosphere, changing the world's climate, altering the heat balance of the whole planet, destroying the world's polar systems, killing the wildlife of icy seas, killing the tropics' coral reefs, raising the level of the sea, turning the oceans acidic, and dissolving shellfish. And as the reefs dissolve and the productivity of oceans and agriculture destabilizes, so will go the food security of hundreds of millions of people."

So let's ponder on this outside with nature, shall we? Ideally somewhere near water. The bathtub will even work. It's all connected. I sensed the water in the bathtub, and even sitting out in the rain one afternoon, absorbing into my body. My body's ultimate need for it because it is mostly water – then the oneness sets in on a very deep and conscious level. It's a fact that we are all biologically and scientifically connected, and we are, essentially the ocean. Once more people sense this, but more so on the positive, good feelings that water is giving them to their psyche, that they are sharing the molecules, then, and only then does a conscious effort take place to want to balance how they treat water, because then, the conscious is fully aware that every drop of water on earth is very much their body, or will somehow cross through the body in some form or another. This level of consciousness wakes up all the other awarenesses of the deepest connection with nature – and, this my friends, is the moment of all truths for a human. This is when many shy away and have to unplug because the hurts or guilt become too overwhelming. What helped me through this was simply remembering that nature gave us the ability to

What we can do is connect the dots in our conscious, but in a balanced way like nature balances itself. Just finding a natural attraction, and fully sensing its being can help make sense of the senselessness here. I encourage that next step through connecting with nature, in your journal, to help you begin to make your peace with it. We can all make peace within ourselves of any negative situation by consciously and deeply sensing and communicating with it on nature's terms – in nature's sensory language, it is about removing all the word and label clutter – and yes, the guilt clutter that usually prevents us from getting too close.

Regarding the oil spill, well, we admit the problem, we admit our participation in it, then hand it over to nature. Our natural senses will take over from there, or our instincts will – the term that many in the biology world use to try to avoid calling our inborn senses natural intelligence, or natural sense (common sense). Dr. Safina is a realist, and creative genius with connecting the dots, which is why I truly admire him. He strives for that balance when he states how we all do love our refrigerators, our cars, and heating. Of course we do. Now we can start tapping into nature for guidance in how to balance our civilized comforts with our psyche. We can stop living the duality of talking about nature, and really walking with it in a comfortable, more balanced way. His recent books "Calling our Wild," and "Beyond Words," are both, well, beyond words! He also founded The Safina Center, completely devoted to our plight for aligning humanity with the natural world.

Everything Carl journey's us through in these, and his other books, continues to solidify, and validate within you that you can make this transformation. It is a transformation of aligning with your natural mind, your "whole mind" as a "whole human."

A new sensory awareness

Now that we have dove deep into many concepts of what I mean by creative sensory intelligence, it is up to you to start listing out which you have, you would like to expand upon and create a strategy for how to get there.

What I found extremely helpful in my journey was to create moments with nature that allowed me to explore, most importantly, sensory connections with the natural world. We will get more into this in our respond phase.

Once we begin to realize that nature, in all the eons, continues –no matter what is going on in our made-up human world. Any scientist will tell you that even if we were to destroy our life source earth – meaning ourselves – nature will still find a way to keep going. Atoms and molecules will continue to interact. Resonating with this can really help us being to find some peace, relieve some anxiousness so we can enjoy our time here while earth is beautiful and is still loving us by unconditionally feeding us our oxygen – helping us make sense of the senseless, well, at least begin to stop making such a big deal about things we physically cannot change at that exact moment.
Over time and practice with this thought process really helps with healing ourselves first and finding our own personal balance. We can really begin to think with and like nature, or

yes, being the habit of asking: what would nature do? (To my biblical friends – even God and Jesus tell us to go to nature because nature is the source of learning).

Now that you have made it this far, through an intense pause phase and this reflection phase, you get to strategize how all this informs your responses to life. The freedom in this journey of discovering who you naturally are, outside the stories throughout the history of humanity, is that you can now be free from that stressful "reactionary" mode that the limited linear thinking kept you trapped in, and move into a more strategic response mode that is authentically aligned with who you are.

Below is the natural connections trail map that might help you try connecting with the natural world to help you discern what does not make sense to you. This could be any specific situation, a relationship, a happening in the world, the loss of a loved one, sickness, or lack of something. Look around your natural area and find a part of it that you can just touch for a moment. It could be a plant, a pet, some water in a pond, or just the wind around you. Now think of one of the things that seem senseless to you.

Really try to connect with the natural connection, and begin to note why you chose it. The texture, color, or shape, and pretend it can tell you exactly why that senseless part is bothering you. What would it say? What parts of it help you minimize hurt, or help to remind you that earth, nature, is still happening in spite of this? As this becomes a habit, you will gradually discover how smart your are, and how smart nature truly is.

As we begin to create our peace of nature through a kinship with it, we create a calm peace of mind., heart and body, our need for safety, belonging and purpose - "home." Please keep with you, the association of "home" in natural world reality, which is... **"HOMEostasis"**

the tendency toward a relatively stable equilibrium between interdependent elements, especially as maintained by physiological processes.

the state of steady internal physical and chemical conditions maintained by living systems. This is the condition of optimal functioning for the organism and includes many variables, such as body temperature and fluid balance, being kept within certain pre-set limits.

A state of balance among all the body systems needed for the body to survive and function correctly.

Natural Connection Trail Map | Natural Self Discovery, copyright 2024

PHASE 3

RESPOND

Where we strategically plan how to intelligently, sensibly respond to situations from our naturally creative, adaptive, collaborative human lens.

Hammock at Eden House, Key West ~ P. Hoke

I frequented this bed and breakfast while I was a Mallory Square Artist. My friends shared my love for weighlessness of the hammocks in gardens of this place of exceptionally nature-centric design, inspiring us to rethink how we do life.

CHAPTER 9

Stepping Away from the Gerbil Wheel

Here we are. Time to walk into the next frontier of natural thinking, and responding to life aligned with our true life force.

We can safely step away from the gerbil wheel we have told we is our only choice. Yet now we know there are so many possibilities, and all we need to do is explore them, and keep learning about ourselves and the natural world we are very much connected to. We also get to discern which stories are working for us, and which are not, and create real strategies that align us with our natural needs, skills, talents, and purpose.

We can choose to stop the circling around and around in a limited thinking that essentially is leading all humans nowhere. Even though it still feels like our current systems are still dominated by the linear thinking, with some dedicated online searches, you will find the hope. There is change coming. In fact, there are plenty of humans out there who are just as sick and tired as you are. Now it is a matter of connecting with them, learning about the amazing research, communities, and organizations that are making a huge difference.

From where we are standing, we simply being the change within ourselves, to discover that calm confidence and strategic responsive way of navigating how we show up.

Creating an informed strategic response

We discussed our natural human needs earlier. This is where the strategy begins. Below is a Pause, Reflect, Respond Map. I combined our brain map words with the circle of human needs and circular relationship with self as whole human in harmony with the natural world and our fellow humans in human world. This map is also combined with the pause, reflect, respond cycle.

For each situation or challenge, or overall where you are today after reading all that you have read here, this map exists purely to inspire you to jot down words and symbols of each element as they ripple out from the human circle of you. This is about zooming out and simplify what our analyzing human minds love to complicate. It also helps to get to our true "why," our purpose

Next, is the Whole Human Check-in Map which has the main five of our natural needs with cups. Fill each cup to the extent you sense each need is fulfilled. Try to write the part of each and why specific ones may or not be as full as you would like. This helps open the door to learning what truly is important to you in the whole picture, and now includes that picture beyond the limited human story world, yet includes the real world of nature.

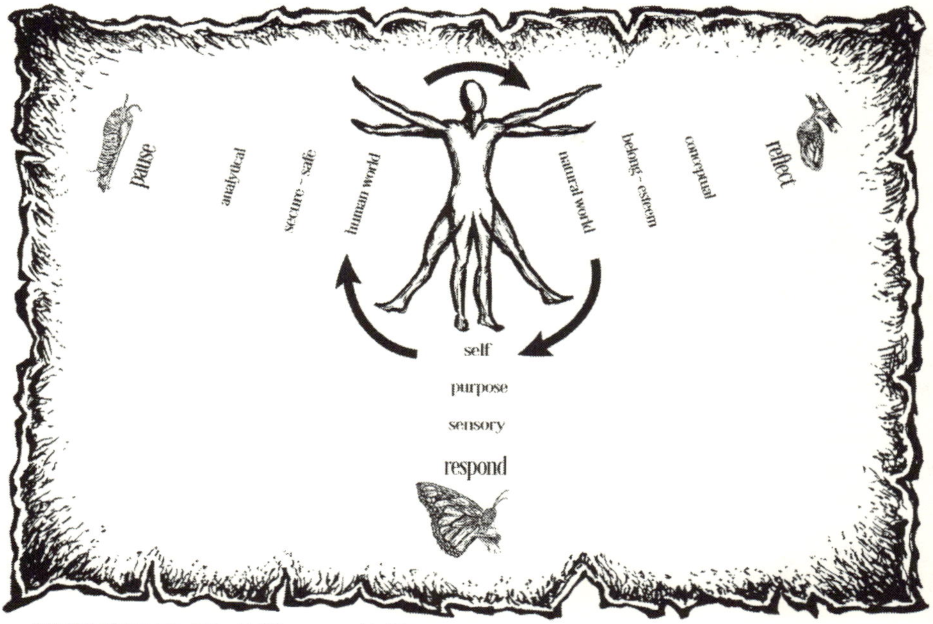

PauseReflectRespond Map | Natural Self Discovery, copyright 2024

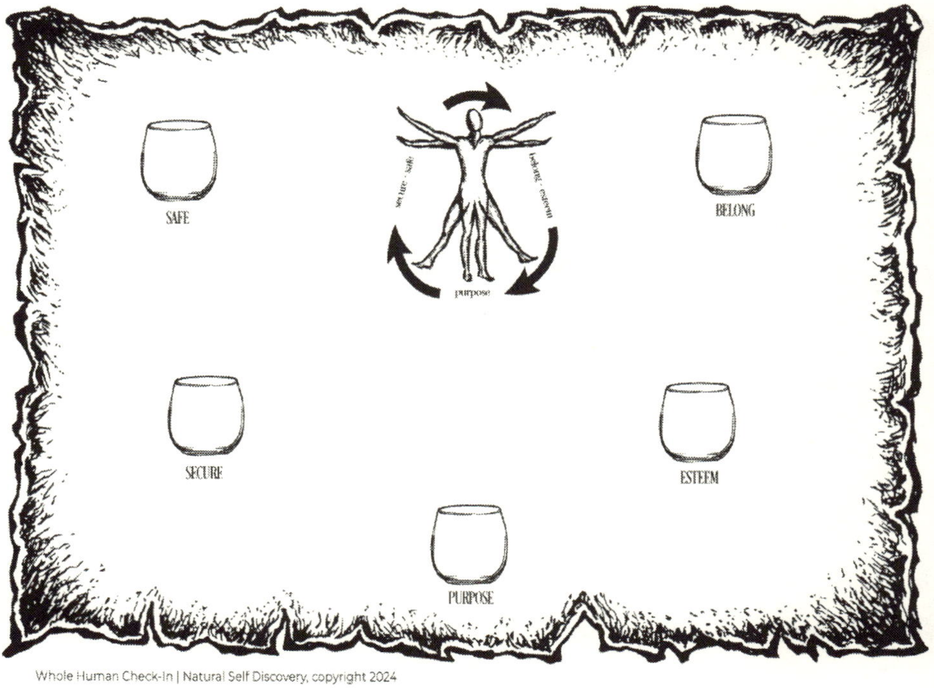

Whole Human Check-In | Natural Self Discovery, copyright 2024

Your "why"

After a full "whole human" awareness session, hopefully you are more solidified in your "why," or closer to knowing if you never really knew what it was, or it changed now that you can look beyond the human realm. Many have shared with me so much yearning to try out painting, or drawing, play an instrument, help or start a non-profit organization, start a business, or to do something that made a difference.

My late spouse scrambled to find his true purpose, and constantly said to me "at least you know what yours is." And he meant it, it is a gift to know. I believe we can all discover it, and I also believe our why can change depending on situations and forces happening around us that move us to respond with our unique talents and skillsets. It is all a matter of staying open, staying sensory aware, and yes, creative!

What's Working, What's not working

Our journey of natural self discovery is a lifelong journey of learning, discerning and responding, yet the beauty of it is the discerning part from a broader lens now What I discover is the main part was the ability to step outside the "gerbil wheel" stories that have led to a lot of harm to humanity and nature. Mostly, the ones that separated us from nature.

As we unpack and sort out gradually a lifetime of stories, and beliefs that are not aligned with who we naturally are, we are going to face some challenges in how we move through them. I found new awarenesses each day, sometimes throughout the day, to the point where just made a habit of jotting them down. I would later map them out with my circle technique (the one earlier where we create circles the size that is relevant to the issue). What can also help is the natural decisions strategy map below. I adapted this one from a recent strategic decision making course. It is essential to stay aligned with your whole human needs check, your natural whole mind in relation to the both the natural world and human world.

This really helps with the big decisions, or discerning which skills to pursue to align with a specific purpose you have always wanted to act on.

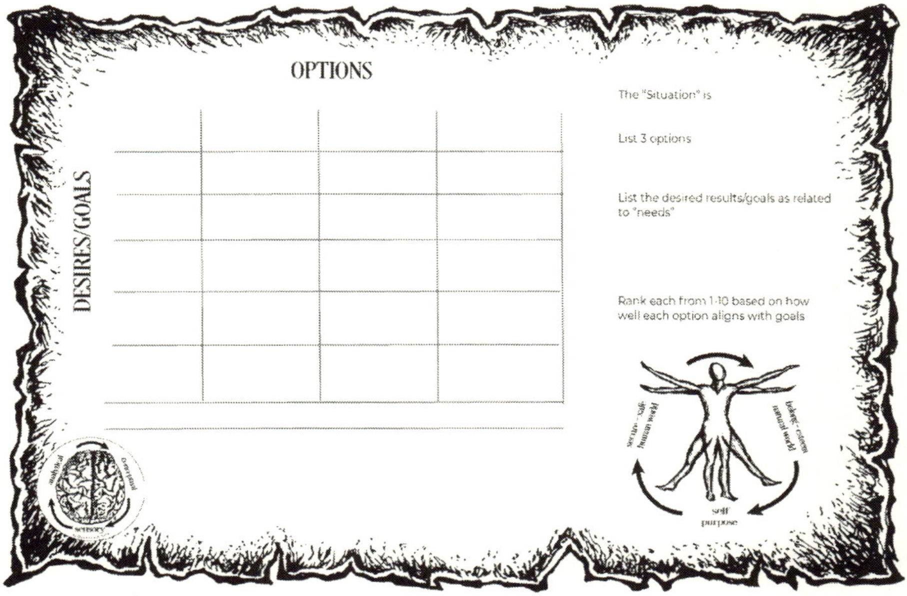

Natural Decisions/Strategy Screen | Natural Self Discovery, copyright 2024

The old stories will keep creeping in

Because I had so much loaded up in my brain and bodily experiences over five decades, it was more than reasonable to expect that it may just take at least half that time to undo the coping thinking patterns that got me this far, yet are now holding me back. I felt it necessary to share this with you so you are prepared. Yet please know just as we actually CAN teach an old dog new tricks (contrary to that bullshit story), we can teach ourselves, and others as we grow in our confidence.

This is where the Pause, Reflect, Respond method has saved my more times than I can count! I use this throughout the day, especially when I feel triggered by some external stimuli. I can now do a quick scan of mind and body along with what is happening around with others and the situation. A rapid situational assessment where the brief pause helps me check myself to develop a response grounded in my natural self (not performing in the old story of trying to fit in). It also helps me not be reactionary to what may be just a brief discomfort because it reminds me of something that happened in the past. Whatever it is, the method works so well, especially because it keeps me aware of others and helps me expand my lens enough to respect everyone has their own frame of reference and their own life experiences with unique stories from those experiences. This also is so helpful with connecting with natural beings in the same sense.

Just having an expanded lens is freedom

What is essential in this part of planning in what ways make sense to you in how you would like to step off that limited world of spinning in a gerbil wheel of thought. This may not require any major changes, just a shift in how you approach your days.

We can get into the old stories that lead to that limited, binary, extreme thinking where we feel we must choose "this or that," when in reality, it may just be a case of re-arranging our routine, or creating a more natural environment in our home, or, simply adding more time with nature into our day.

This is a gradual process, and from what I experienced, was simply having the expanded lens was liberating. It is what led me to spend dedicate time in learning what was not taught to me. It meant digging for truths that were omitted from my conditioning,

We all have to do what makes sense for achieving "homeostasis," whether that means within ourselves, our home life, relationships, work life, or leading people or projects in our community. And as long we remember that we now have nature as our ultimate teacher, and we now have opened our minds that there is an entirely new world of creative intelligence which we can now access to, stepping off the old gerbil wheel thinking is not so daunting after all. The following two pages have the key maps which might help you along.

Pause Reflect Respond Check-in | Natural Self Discovery, copyright 2024

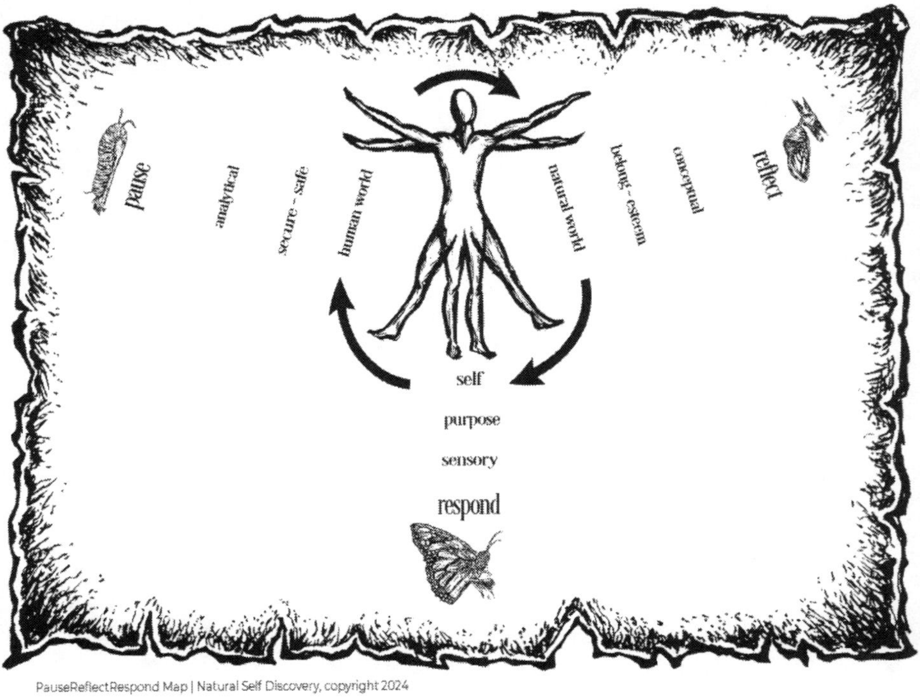

PauseReflectRespond Map | Natural Self Discovery, copyright 2024

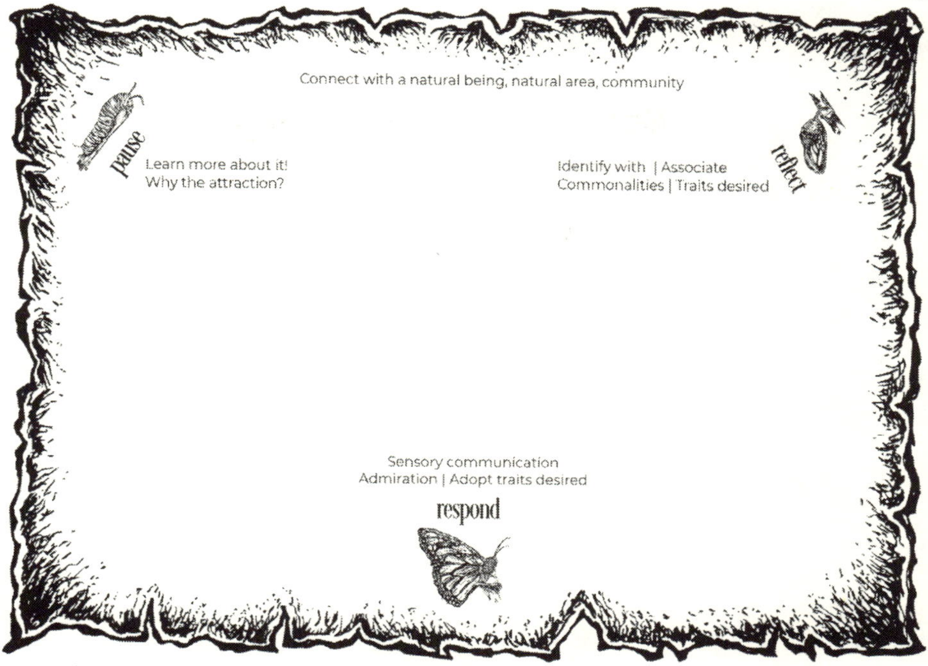

Natural Connection Trail Map | Natural Self Discovery, copyright 2024

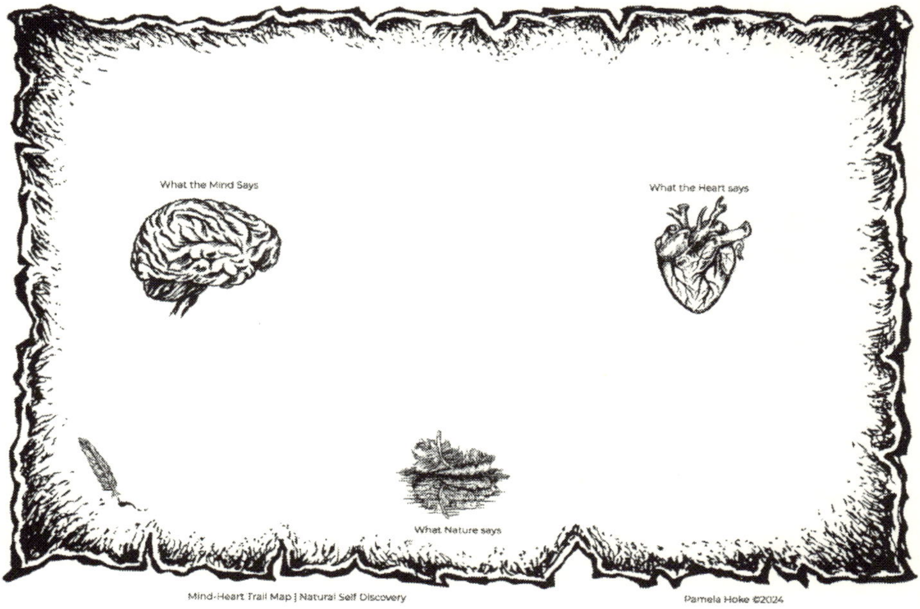

Mind-Heart Trail Map | Natural Self Discovery

Pamela Hoke ©2024

Oak Journey ~ P. Hoke

I grew up with a huge Oak Tree in my back yard, which became a friend and place of solace for me. This expressies the energy, love and inspiration II feel whenever I encounter oak leaves, especially during the incredible natural transitions of autumn.

CHAPTER 10

Becoming the Strongest Oak

"When we long for life without difficulties, remind us that oaks grow strong in contrary winds and diamonds are made under pressure."

~ Peter Marshall

This limited thinking has really has taken away our ability to embrace ambiguity, to fear anything that take us out of our comfort zones, to she from challenges and facing adversities more than anything. It has also led us to avoid grief (around many changes in life) purely out of the discomfort or inconvenience taking time to process grief causes.

The old stories keeps our brains in that habitual loop to prioritize our need for comfort and security to an imbalanced, unhealthy need to snuggle into that safe spot - which actually disables us later on. One of my favorite saying I picked up in my support circles is "whatever we resist, persists." I had mentioned this golden nugget earlier, yet here it is again. Because it is the ultimate truth. Especially when we do our zoom out and explore of the entirety of humanity and planet relationship as it has become. There are still those last-gaspers clinging to resisting even looking at the issue, or thinking by ignoring it or delaying action actually is not going to cost them dearly. I can say this with ultimate confidence only because I have reviewed multiple budgets and cost benefit analyses recently. Many of the companies and individuals who are directly resisting the shifts are actually now fiscally irresponsible because the costs of simply resisting making transitions now are leading to their actual demise beyond what any spreadsheet can demonstrate. I really hope that more shareholders would simply sue the biggest culprits contributing to the accelerated pace of destroying our habitat for being fiscally irresponsible - because, according to the law, they could. The companies are not looking out for the long-term interests and security that the company will even sustain itself through the changes that are coming, let alone preparation for supply chains to continue to be disrupted. I could go on and on about this from my recent studies, especially in greenhouse gas accounting and sustainability assessments, combined with decades of studying each year's Climate Report.

This principle goes for individuals who resist any life transition of any kind. It is all about processing the entire cycle of transitions. The strongest oaks know the importance of transitions, and is why they can grow so big! If you look to nature, it is constantly shifting and moving. It inhabitants, with the exception of us humans clinging to our comforts, are open and ready for these shifts and changes. Nature shows us each minute how to go with the flow of what life hands us, but more importantly, teaches us strength.

I will forever have an attachment to oak trees because of the one that supported me and gave me strength through my childhood, yet recently the strong oaks on the University of

Washington campus were always there to remind me I could meet the challenge of graduate school, along with all the changes that were happening within me from that journey.

Nature also showed me how to process the grief of my husband Tim's passing, and so many other losses. The point of truly flowing through grief, whether it is loss of a loved one, loss of a job, change of a job, a move even if it is to somewhere better (there is a loss to process)...loss from changes within a community or organization. That begins with making space to acknowledge and grieve so that there is a chance to transition into that weird in-between space where the adjustments can actually happen into the new "normal."

The butterfly transition mandates that cocoon time, yet it requires the pause period to really look at the situation so the loss or mental processing happens to prepare fully for the "next," whatever the next is.

I will say this over and over again, for any grief processing, or any transition, either individually, or as a group, going to nature and creating is what has always been the path, Both open the space for experiencing transition on that sensory level, that depth of thought and expression that assures growth into the next stronger, better and definitely more "whole."

A nature-based strategy to any situation

As we begin to learn to go to nature and immerse in creative exploration, there are specific strategies that can be applied to assist in this specific transition. Any shift requires strategy.

Next are some trail maps which I have found incredibly supportive in helping me create not only personal adaptations, yet also in planning organization shifts in my businesses. They are adapted from proven methods from Dobel and Day strategic mapping models.

The first is a Forces and Pressures Map. The reason is because when we embark upon changes, especially in our current human-centric thinking that is still predominantly resistant to change, we need to have an idea of who are our true allies, resources and support systems. We also need to assess which resources and support networks/individuals or groups can best help us in our situation or mission.

The next is a Natural Alignment Strategy Map. This can help once you have an idea of support and resources to ensure through visualization of the whole picture, that you have thought through all possibilities.

Then, we can add in the Natural Decision Map again. With all three of these, you have a path towards creating a strategy toward your goals in your new natural self lens, and the expanded lens of your purpose and alignment within both human and natural worlds.

I hope these might help you feel like you do have the strong support to become the strongest oak. .

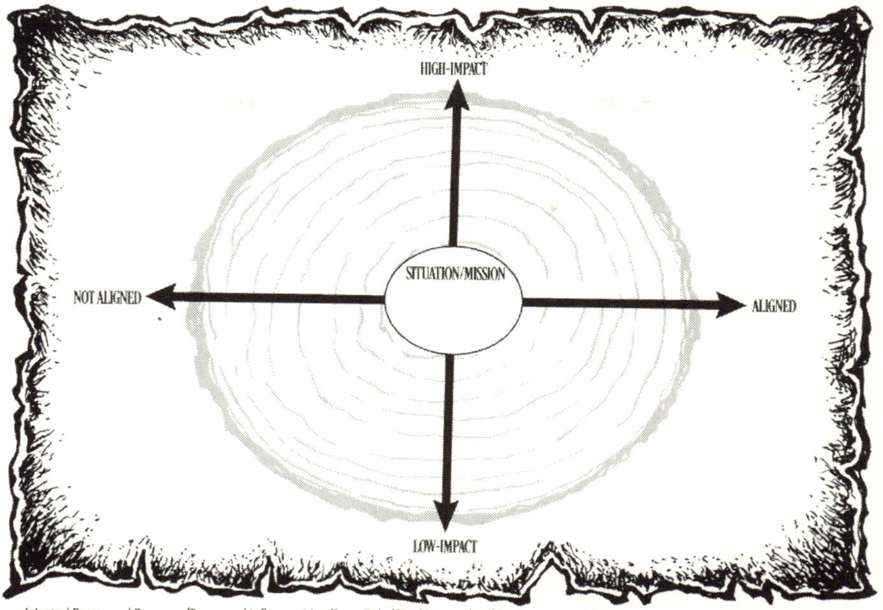

Adapted Forces and Pressures/Power and Influence Map (from Dobel/Day) | Natural Self Discovery, copyright 2024

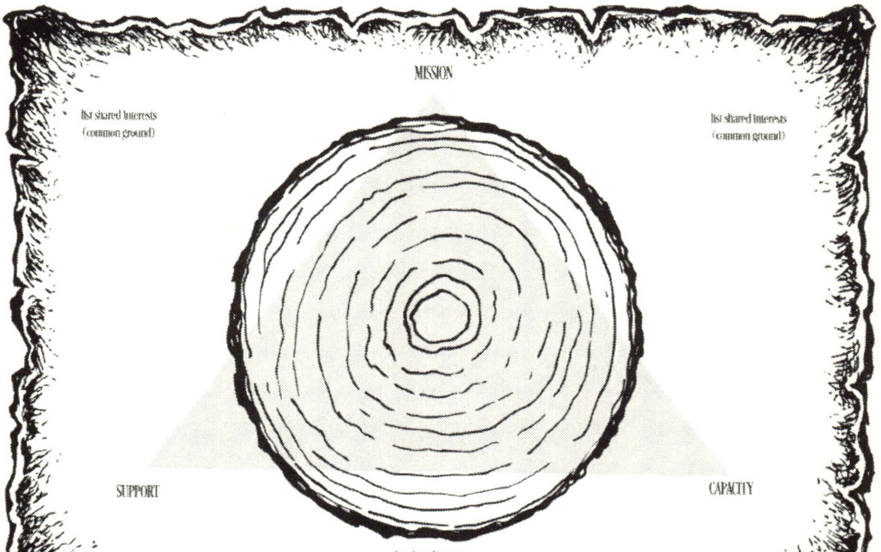

Natural Alignment Strategy Map | Natural Self Discovery, copyright 2024

adaption from Dobel/Day Mapping

A nature connecting activity that might inspire

This one is simple. Go to your nature space of the moment and jot down the things going on around you that matter most to you. You know, the ones that nag at you with a sense of "someone should do something about that."
Now, sit quietly with this list and let your natural attractions around you inspire you to sense and feel what you can reasonably and peacefully take responsibility for – either a letter, a phone call, or if ready, begin playing with that career path or life change you always talked about doing, but denied yourself (perhaps for the sake of having more stuff or stature with peers or because you have been after someone else's approval or that of your peers).

Begin "playing out the scenario while in your natural spot. Look the natural beings around you for inspiration. You may discover a peaceful, more loving way of expressing some long buried feelings to someone that you have buried and avoided. You might create an incredible idea for your current job that applies what is important to you regarding the environment or health. You might have fun listing out your new life as an explorer, educator, artist or musician. Let nature be the sounding board – the goal is to have fun playing with new plans and creative ways to speak your mind and begin acknowledging what your part of the web of life really is.

What is amazing about playing this all out, is the creativity begins to flow, the courage also grows within because nature shows you that you can be whatever it is you want to be –

because, while with nature, which is the real reality by the way – you are not being judged or criticized, only encouraged to be your natural self.   We can begin to learn how to balance being our natural selves in nature where nature doesn't point a finger at us so we can practice and visualize how we can balance in the human-made modern world.

Here is the Decision Strategy Map to add to the maps to help in your strongest oak strategy.

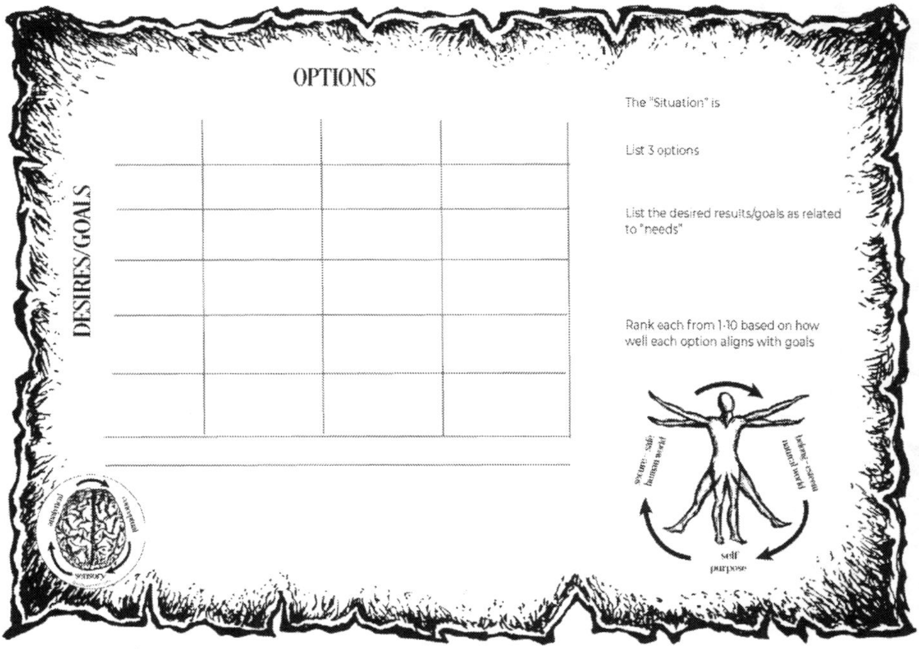

Natural Decisions/Strategy Screen | Natural Self Discovery, copyright 2024

Humpback Whale Vibes ~ P. Hoke

I woke up from my fall retreat San Juan Island Park campground to get to see this Humpback Whale far in the distance, and could feel its life vibrations as it splashed away. Whales show me how to trust in nature, respect my place in it and look to larger species like whales for wisdom.

CHAPTER 11

How to Let Go and Let Nature

"We can gently move forward individually - peacefully and respectfully of ourselves, others and nature. We can let go of toxic thoughts and people with love, wish them the best, send good vibes, then trust nature's course."

- me

Learning to create nature-aligned responses to life helps like start to feel more natural. I can attest to this, especially when I look back at how the rushed modern mindset of reactionary mode to everything. It was exhausting! I think of how some of my nature connections (the animals I identify with) might see us humans. I envision them thinking "what the heck is wrong with these bald creatures?"

Let's circle back to earlier when we briefly went over the situational assessment of the human relationship with the natural world. The. Add in the visual of our imbalanced analytical minds in the harried flurry of a gerbil wheel to nowhere - the "nowhere" of where we scurry for finite resources, when earth can provide an abundance infinite resources in it's intelligent, regenerative design.

That is, we would just step out of the way and let Earth do it's regenerative process. We all saw the evidence during the COVID pandemic that when humans are out of the way, nature does its regenerative process. And there is now an abundance of humans who have done all the research and created brilliant strategies over the past decades who have the trails towards mirroring Earth's genius regenerative design. So we essentially have left to do, with the technology and methods in place, is now tell others we need to get let go and let nature once again be our original energy. With that kept in the back our minds, we surely have a shared mission, a hopeful purpose that can recreate that zest, re-ignite our drive, and that deep passion for life that we crave. We actually get to live in just that purpose, because biologically speaking, it is a core our human needs: safety and security.

After beginning to fully re-engage my natural thought processes and reclaim my intrinsic relationship with nature, I have found a way to trust in nature. The natural processes and life cycles however cannot do what they need to do with humans constantly interfering to the point that we actually cause more harm. If we were to truly apply any mindset to our naturally collaborative thinking we would start with the key medical phrase "first do no harm."

The other phrase I keep close is the one from the first Jurassic Park movie....we always look at what we can do, yet never ask "should we." I would be remiss if I didn't state once again how we really need to examine our human superiority complex which is now deeply implanted in our imbalanced left-brain dominant thinking of most modern humans. At least those who are leading currently.

In discussing leadership, we can learn from the emerging adaptive leadership frameworks and methods which do include pathways toward using our whole minds and acknowledges our whole humanness.

The first part is learning to lead ourselves, so we are able to lead others, and therefore lead change. This simple mindset is also cyclical, like our new tools. All the tools try to stay in three's because not only are natural attracted to patterns, keeping things in 3's when it comes to tasks appeals to our left analytical minds, they keep that part of brain occupied, so our sensory creative minds can be free to sense the "whole" and ideate real solutions. Kind of sneaky, yes? Yet, a strategy that holds well when it comes to undoing a centuries long habit of billions of beings.

My favorite nature analogy when it comes to learning how to navigate life with this expanded lens and way of thinking is the hermit crab visualization. I first heard it from Melodie Beattie in her Language of Letting Go book. If a hermit crab is willing to leave the old shell it has outgrown, meaning going through that vulnerable stage of being exposed to elements, it will die. I keep this in the back of my mind whenever I need to let go of my old stories that keep me in fear.

Letting go is a method that works, especially in the proven new leadership methods. What we thought was leadership, we now know is ineffective. Human Resources, as we call it in our commodity mindset, are intricate ecosystems of their own, and because of our infinitely unique identities and life journey experiences, along with the biases and stories accumulated during the first decades of our lives, there is never going to be a one-size-fits-all with any group, organization, method, process or family path.

This is the ridiculous part of the old leadership story that we must let go. From this thought train, as I let go of this process of natural self discovery our there, is a list of the adaptive leadership books I had the privilege of studying, and I hope they might help you to create your leadership journey with a reclaimed part of your mind and connected to the natural world. A path where you lead yourself into the life you always knew was yours to live. From there, all have to do is show in this mindset, and the rest naturally will happen, through the energy we exude. (Keep in mind, we learn how to efficient from the natural world - just observe any animal and you will see just how well nature knows efficiency from the self-sustaining mindset).

Here are just a few of my favorites which have helped me immensely in the entire process of letting go of old ideas and learning new ones. Especially during my own recent "chrysalis" phase, in graduate school. I let go and allowed that messy process to just happen. I let go and kept showing up as the most present whole human possible. I took care of myself as my intelligent natural body led me to, outside the old, ineffective non-sustaining story loops, and made room for the new. There are so many more, yet these we major go-to's as I developed my unique strategy to navigate my trail moving forward -in both my personal, professional relationships and my renewed kinship with Earth.

Ask for More, 10 Questions to Negotiate Anything
by Alexandria Carter
Any and All recent research, and the concepts available online regarding Collaborative Governance will assist you in your individual strategy, family strategy, organizational and community or team strategy - I cannot stress this enough. Get creative!
Drive by Daniel Pink ~ Richard Louv's books, Carl Safina's books
Brene Brown books ~ Mel Robbins books
Farsighted by Steven Johnson
Managing Transitions by William Bridges
Braiding Sweetgrass by Robin Wall Kimmerer
The Artist;s Way by Julia Cameron
The Spell of the Sensuous by David Abram
Don't you know Who I Am, by Ramani Durvasula
Sum of Us by Heather McGee
The Language of Letting Go - Melody Beattie

These are just a glimpse, yet I sense these are the ones that need to be listed here for now. Also, as I stay the course in creating a habit of learning to think like and with nature through creating nature connections, in staying plugged into the sensory natural world, I found Bernadette King's award winning Ark Set continues to help me strengthen my bonds in my new way of relating to the natural world. This does require ditching the old stories that create fear of the ancient wisdom of spirit animals, and tarot. As a descendant of natural healers of Scotland, I now know that those stories were created to separate us from our connection with the natural world. These cards and book are my go to for sensing and learning the traits of the animal world, finding the traits and support needed for each project, task or next transformation.

A few more notes on letting go

I also keep a mantra at the core of my mind, which was inspired by the rescued owls I got to work with in teaching art to students in my Nature as Muse program. I love the way owls calmly turn their head completely around is the smoothest response after their situational assessment of humans acting irrationally or disrespectfully. What I gathered from this is "stay in my own lane." We cannot control others' behaviors, we can try to nudge or influence (which only effective is we are leading by example), the rest is up to them. We can assess first if there is clear and present danger like an owl would, yet once that occurs and it is merely a fellow human with hurts and currently unable to hear any message, the most loving things we can do is stay in our lane, so they get to learn what they need to learn on their own.

It is not only inefficient in the world of nature to poke into other's business, we know to well from the dominant linear mindset of how this intrusive, disrespectful, paternalizing behavior it is ineffective and unhealthy. When we poke into other's business and have not truly handled our own business, we are meddling to avoid handling our own business.

We can also stop the finger pointing, the old blaming and shaming just keeps us in that habitual loop of the mindset which has caused all the problems. Yes, we assess the root of the problem and the cause, yet with a full assessment, valuing the space to process all lenses, explore and create all possibilities, we can then strategically respond in a way that will be more effective. Do we need to speak up, call out atrocities and unjust situations? Hell yes. However, we can do this strategically because there is a lot at stake, and we know we need to ensure the message lands effectively at this point. Too much is at stake. And there are a whole lot of stakeholders with a whole lot of embedded stories, biases, and different frames of references that we need to stay mindful of if we are going to get through.

Finger pointing will gets us nowhere, we see over and over again on social media that it only perpetuates division. Go to any article on strategic negotiations and there is an abundance of research on the most important element: making sure whoever you are engaging with feels seen and heard. It is a primal human need, even when that person might be stuck in their old stories, their limited lens, How else do we invite them into our lens yet to "invite" with warmth?

Our old blaming and shaming patterns keep us stuck in the extreme analytical thinking cycle never ends well for relationships. This is where nature and the creative process can really help us create new strategies. Plus, it is rather fun (in a snarky way) and fulfilling to know we are moving towards a solution. Many of us know this too well with relationship that ended, or we found ourselves with fewer friends, or family experiencing a judgmental asshole. Also, alienating ourselves in this manner does not set the tone of natural collaborative energy. If we are genuinely in a process of fulfilling our natural human needs, and moving towards living a more abundant, passionate life full of connections grounded in aligned purpose, it does require a habit of strengthening a sense of self, others and the world around us.

Here is the disconnect map that might serve as a reminder of our situation in relation to the "whole" of the natural world... I created this map to remind me of the deeply embedded systemic thinking of modern humanity that was designed to keep us separate, and divided: from our natural selves, others and especially nature. I found this helps me re-frame the reality, yet keeps me grounded in the "long game" strategy. I hope it

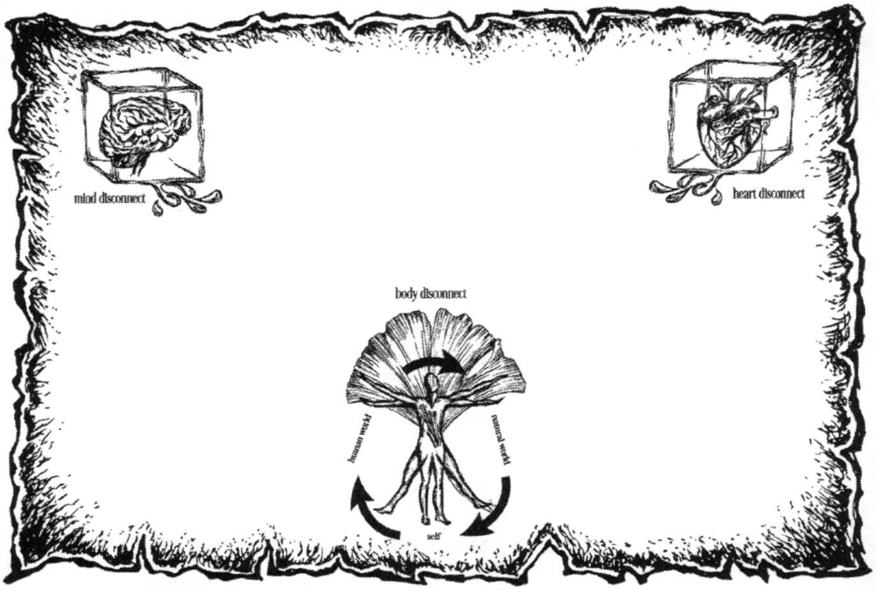

Disconnect Map | Natural Self Discovery, copyright 2024

helps you!

On the note of staying in our own lane: yes, we can speak our minds, yet perhaps learn a balanced approach in our full sensory awareness mindset plugged into nature, of a calm, confident process of calling-out and calling-in, depending on the situation and the humans involved. We can learn to do this in the most respectful and compassionate manner – then move on! Let go, and let nature take its course. What helps me most times when anyone is being hurtful or just plain making bad decisions for themselves or the rest of us on this planet, is, accept that they have a learning journey to experience themselves. We all know the reality of how we could only learn to walk ourselves by doing it - experiencing all the bumps and bruises. The most loving thing we can do is let go and let nature teach them.

We are, after all, of and with nature – we know we can be our naturally sensory, intelligent and creative selves no matter what anyone says. No one can take that away from us. The next chapter includes some additional ways to help you get started on your new journey of natural self discovery.

FINAL NOTE: all us need to file this way, from individuals, to educators and leaders.

1. Let go by going to Nature : Learn from the experts in sustaining life

2. Let go by going to Indigenous People and Cultures:
Learn from the experts in effective balanced human relationship

Lighten Up Feather 1 ~ P. Hoke

A recent reflective feather expressing a pause moment after I encountered this beautiful feather while embracing the solace with nature during the pandemic

CHAPTER 12

Riding Life a Little Lighter and Wiser

"I'm too busy!" aka
"It's not aligned with my priorities"

Ah. Our well used excuse in an effort to "be nice." This gem is deeply rooted in our modern societal norms, yet if we really zoom on this one, it removes any chance of establishing intimacy, trust and genuine honest connection with others. I have been slowly learning how to respond with not having to explain myself fully to others, yet share honestly when I am being asked to do something which does not align with my whole human experience, or if it is at a time when I have already committed to something. Riding life lighter begins with us being true to ourselves, and just in doing that, being the change of the false "niceties" of the old stories keeping us separated, and demonstrating kindness through truth. That is how we know who aligns with us naturally, also. The lightening up is about realizing we do deserve to be in community with those who share our interests, and the only way we can do that is be honest about our interests. As I grew in an expanded lens, I love the new expanded community and lenses of others I get to learn from and engage with - lenses of different cultures and life experiences. Lighter and wiser. Feeling more connected, and confident from all that I am learning. I want this for all us.

Now that we are beginning a path to discovering what our natural selves desire, we get to be more discerning of where our energy goes during each 24 hours of each day. Hopefully you are discovering some more truths about yourself from nature, and navigating with some of your own strategy maps of how to reach what truly aligns inside you as a human being, not the human "doing" of those old outdated stories imposed upon you. Yes, I get it, you are amazingly busy, in your overwhelmingly busy schedule you have created for yourself. I get it because I still find myself asking where the last 24 hours went, where the last week went, and where the heck did the last year go? In order to help us do what we can to grasp our nature dosage, I created a quick list of things that can realistically be done to get your quick "nature fix," either to break up the day, take pause during a difficult exchange with other humans, or just because you need the pick-me-up!

"The Nature Fix, Why Nature Makes us Happier, Healthier and more Creative" by Florence Williams is a major boost to keep us on track. Also, head to Mel Robbins' podcast, she is the expert on effective way to hack our old thinking patterns! Her "Make It Happen" series helped me finish this new version of Natural Self Discovery, and her new "Let them" book addresses exactly what we are discussing here.

Don't we desire to float through our days like a feather on air? Well, we can be in the reality of physics of the natural world here, and accept that all cycles require a constant movement of calm, friction, then the new form. There is an infinite realm of possibilities of what happens in the in-between stage of anything. Once we accept this, we do become more willing to get comfortable in the uncomfortable "messy" stage - the chrysalis stage. That is where the real learning happens, the real exploration and possible solutions arrive.

It is possible, but it means creating a habit. And I need to be honest here, although positive affirmations and positive thinking has helped so many, we must be in reality that if imbalanced in the extreme thinking (just like an addict in extreme dependence on a substance), we create a wall to processing all the parts of life experiences. Which, yes, natural law requires the whole package - the good, the not so good, and the ugly. No mud, no lotus. We can teach ourselves to ride through the mud, or balance above water if our feather is being weighed down.

If it helps, I view going to nature for support as if I was taking my happy pill! The only side effects I have noticed is some people stare at my funny if I touch a leaf sporadically, or suddenly move closer to a bird...but hey, it is a lot less harmful than the alternative substances we humans have concocted!

I hope all these thoughts might help get you started, and inspire your creative juices to flow out your own innovative "nature fixes." The point is...Nature is around us to tap in whenever we need it, and we finally aware that we can decide when to "say when" and when to say where, and for how long. Knowing nature this way is invigorating, refreshing, and our personal happy place whenever we need it. There is an abundance of professionals now teaching both connecting with nature, and sharing the artistic process. It is now simply a matter of valuing these activities as if our lives depend upon them, because essentially they do.

So, this part is the parting.

I sensed you have read my rambling long enough, and I am ready to hit the studio and paint heart and brain images with melting ice around them.

As a wrap up, please refer to the back pages with all the maps we reviewed throughout the book. These are available for free on my website at PamelaHoke.com. And no, I am not even going to ask for your email. I understand the onslaught of emails. My hope is you simply share your experiences online, tag me on social media, and definitely direct message me! I am so curious about how anything here helped you, and curious as to ways I can adapt the maps, the NSD process. I am open to feedback, and collaboration with the process as it is something new, and I definitely need my fellow humans to bring new lenses and ideas to expand upon it, so it can help us adapt into our next frontier of maturity as a species.

Here's few tidbits, I am sure I will add more as I go along this journey with you

PAUSE, REFLECT, RESPOND (and REPEAT) cycle for all situations ~ Try the check-in maps to stay your course ~ Try the 24 Hour Trail Map with the 3's simple concept ~ Practice with Nature, and yes, draw/doodle with nature and learn your two new universal

languages of nature and art! ~ Rehearse communications with Nature ~ Grieve with Nature ~ Natural light before Digital Light Quiet moments with Nature first! ~ Gratitude goes a long way Keep your Values list handy to always ask "does it align?"

Go discover "your" people, natural attraction energy goes a long way, and stay open to new lenses, cultures and communities.

Now the fun part – create your nature "fixes" in your nature journal, create your maps and strategies! Begin to document how certain parts of nature support you, or help you identify with your thoughts or feelings. Then discover others who can do the same. Develop creative, subtle ways to plug into the planet to keep you creatively sensory intelligent, and more aware of your surroundings and others than you've ever been.

Thank you for spending some of your priceless life moments with me, and I do hope we get to connect along our shared interests in normalizing the societal reclaiming our whole humanness in our restored relationship with nature and our natural creative sensory intelligences.

Harmony for People and Planet,

Love, Pam

BIBLIOGRAPHY

Abram, David PhD, The Spell of the Sensuous, Perception and Language in a More than Human World 1996 Pantheon Books

Ackerman, Diane, An Alchemy of the Mind, 2004, Scribner

Beattie, Melody - Language of Letting Go, 1990, Hazelton

Bridges, William PhD and Susan, Managing Transitions, 2016Da Capo Press

Brown, Brene', Braving the Wilderness, 2017, Penguin Random House, Daring Greatly, and The Gifts of Imperfection

Bunch, Will, After the Ivory Tower Falls, How College Broke the American Dream and Blew Up our Politics, and How to Fix It, 2022 Harper Collins

Cameron, Juile, The Artist's Way, Heart Steps

Carroll, Lewis, Alice in Wonderland

Carter, Alexandra, Ask For More, 10 Questions to Negotiate Anything,

Cohen, Michael, PhD, EdD - Reconnecting with Nature, The Web of Life Imperative, Natural Systems Thinking Process

DeWall, Frans, The Age of Empathy

Durvasula, Ramani S., PhD, Don't You Know Who I am?, How to Stay Sane in an Era of Narcisssim, 2019, Post Hill Press, It's Not You

Earle, Sylvia, The World is Blue, 2009, National Geographic

Edwards, Betty, Drawing on the Right Side of the Brain, 1987, Tarcher/ Putnam Press

Florida, Richard, Rise of the Creative Class

Gore, All, Inconvenient Truth, 2006, Rodale

Heginworth, Ian Siddons - Environmental Arts Therapy and the Tree of Life

Johnson, Steven, Farsighted, 2018 John Murray Publishers

Kimmerer, Robin Wall, Braiding Sweetgrass

Louv, Richard, The Nature Principle, Last Child in the Woods

McGhee, Heather, Sum of Us

Pink, Daniel - A Whole New Mind, Why Right-Brainers will rule the world, Drive, The Power of Regret

Robinson, Sir Ken, The Element, 2009, Penguin Books

Rosczak, Theodore, Ecopsychology

Rosenberg, Marhsall B., NonViolent Communication, 2015 Puddle Dancer Press

Safina, Carl, Beyond Words, A Sea in Flames: The Deepwater Horizon, Voyage of the Turtle: In Pursuit of the Earth's Last Dinosaur

Smith, Penelope, Animals Speak, and Animal Talk, Atria Books

Tolle, Ekhart - A New Earth: Awakening your Life's Purpose, 2006, Plume

Van der Kolk, Bessel, The Body Keeps Score

Williams, Florence, The Nature Fix, Why Nature Makes us Happier, Healthier, and More Creative, 2017, W.W. Norton & Company

Wilson, Edward O., The Social Conquest of Earth, and On Human Nature

Wohlleben, Perter, The Hidden Life of Trees

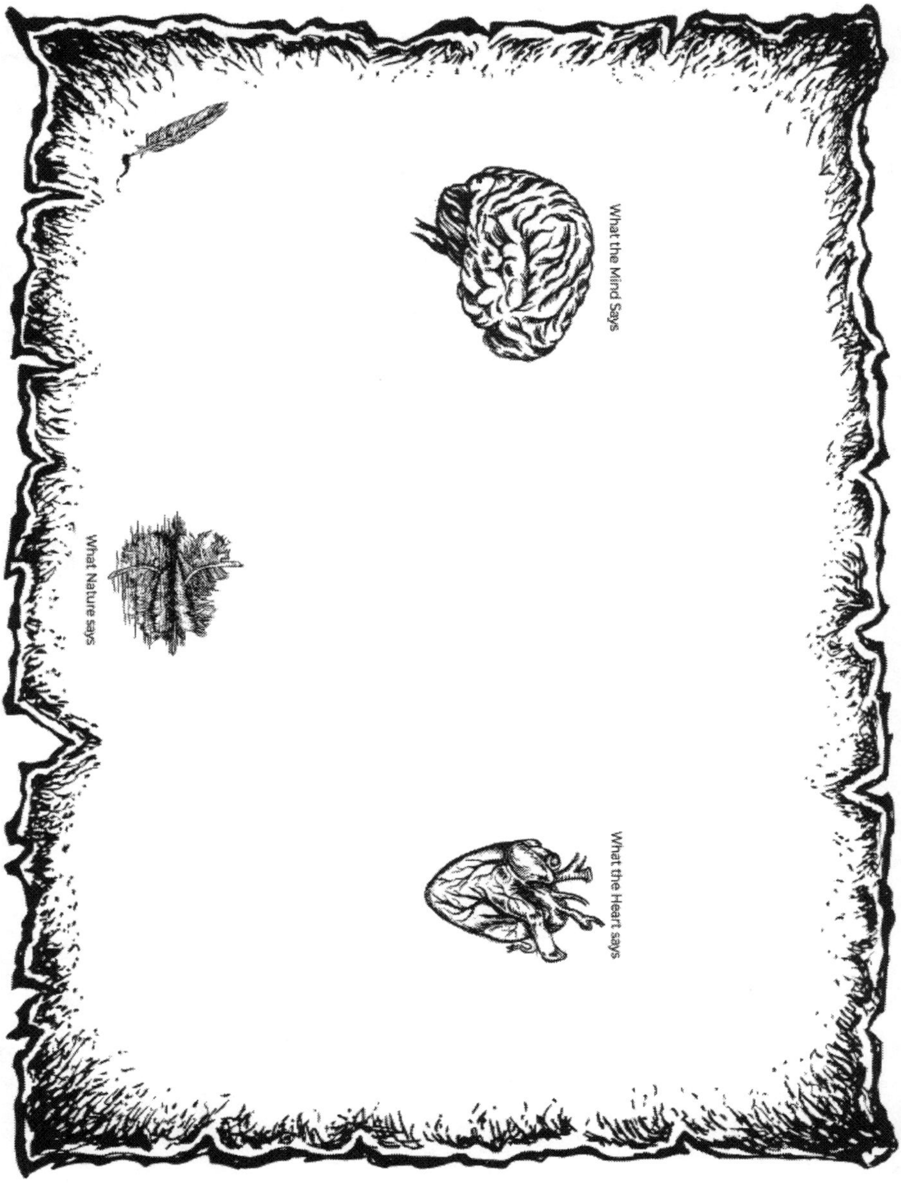

Mind-Heart Trail Map | Natural Self Discovery

Pamela Hoke ©2024

ADDITIONAL TOOLS - the Maps

Downloadable PDF's are available at pamelahoke.com

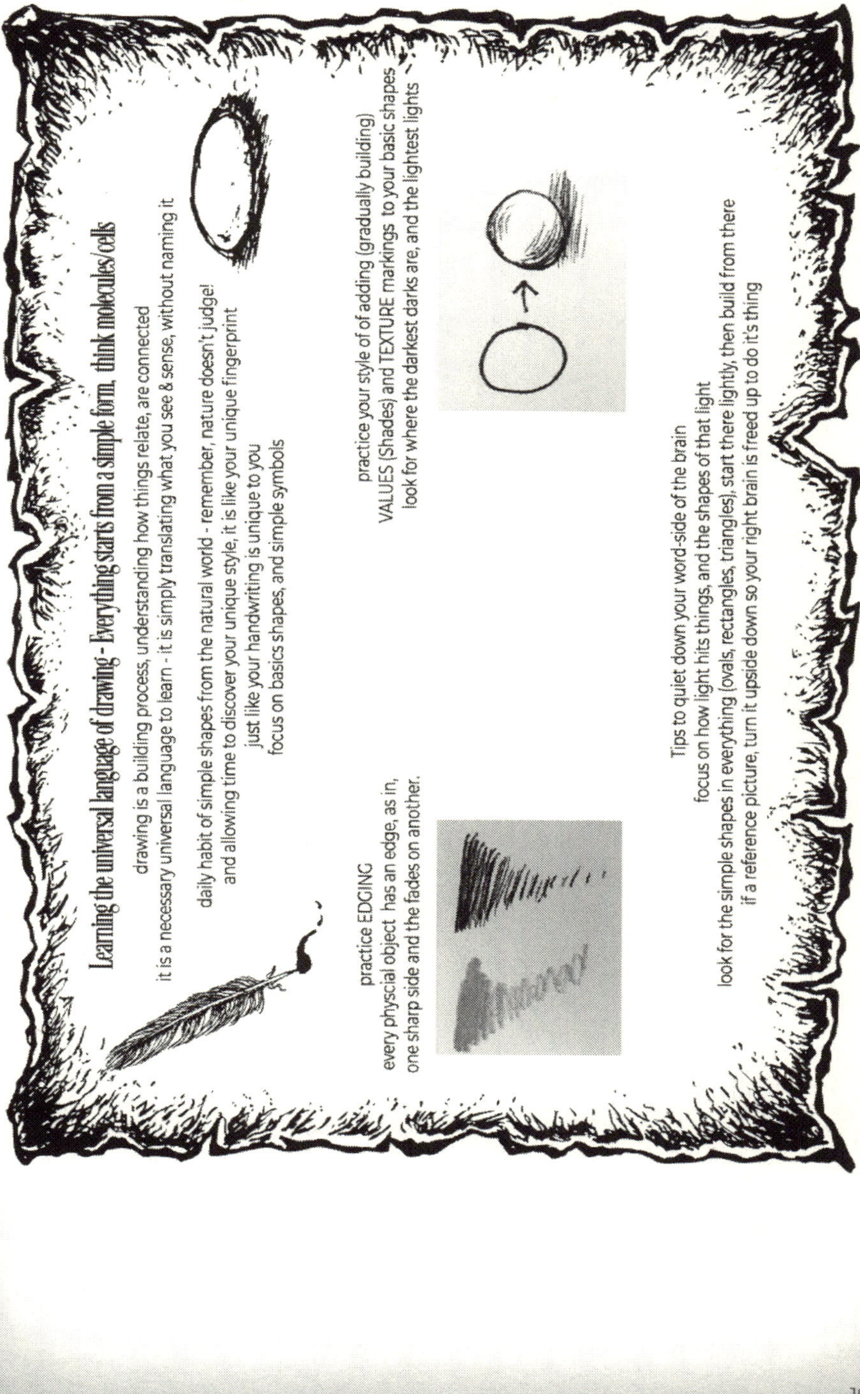

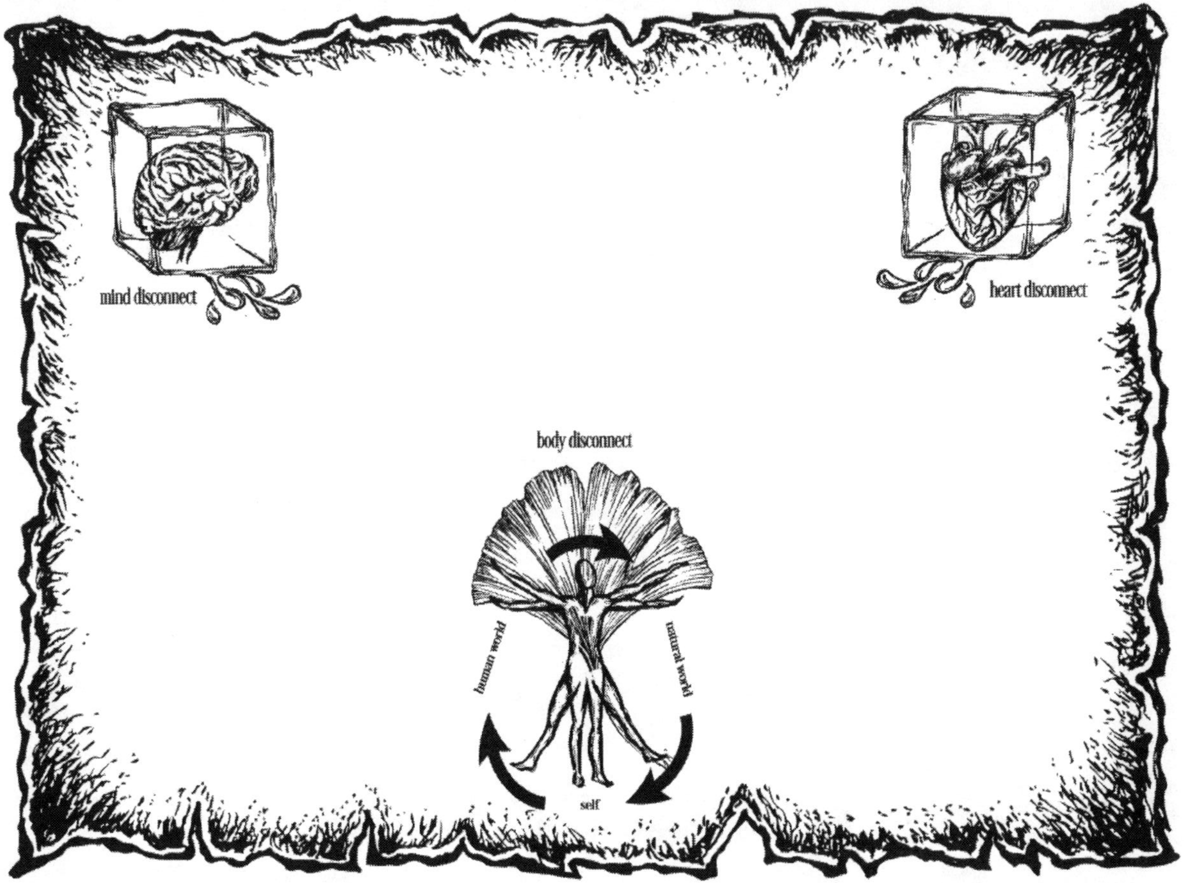

Disconnect Map | Natural Self Discovery, copyright 2024

mid-day

natural contact
mind/body check-in
pause-reflect-respond

the Main 3

which "need" ? S, R or P
(security|relationships|purpose)

____

____

____

morning

natural contact
mind/body check-in
pause-reflect-respond

evening

natural contact
mind/body check-in
pause-reflect-respond

Whole Human Check-In | Natural Self Discovery, copyright 2024

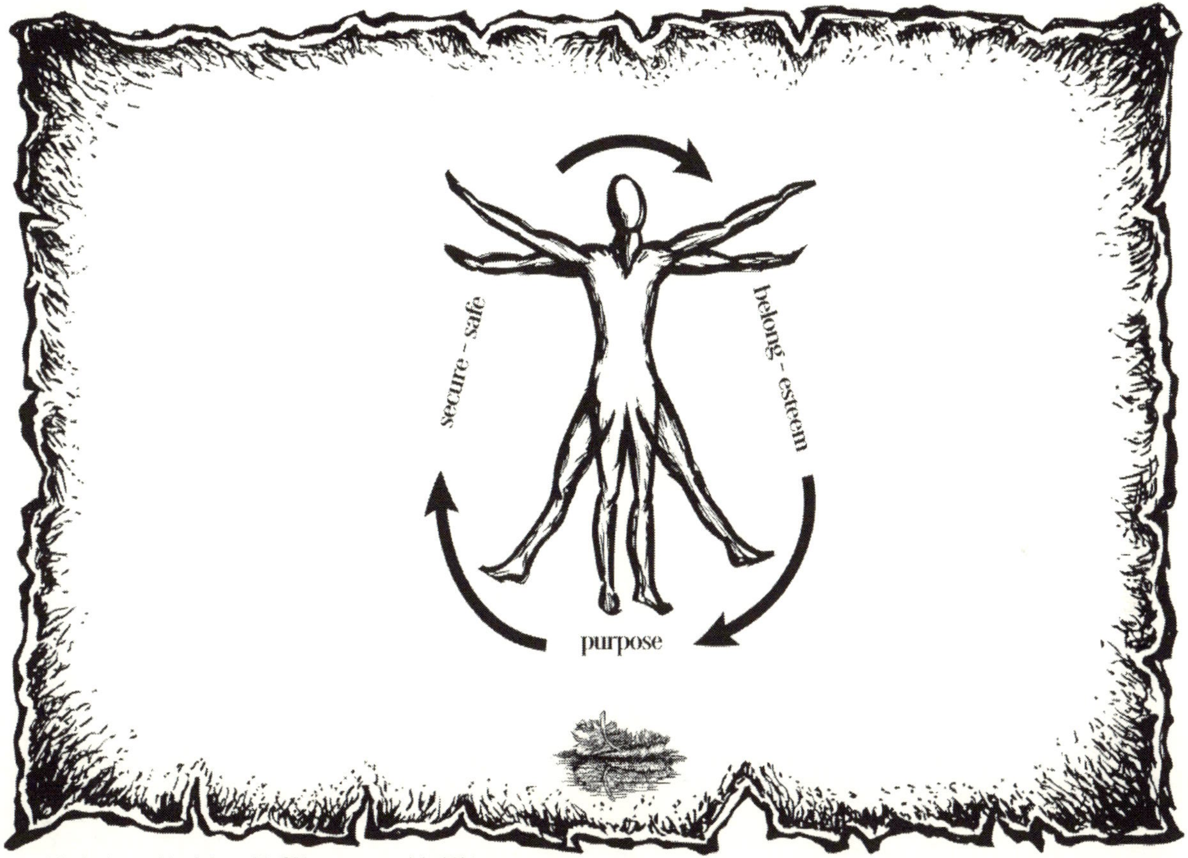

secure - safe
belong - esteem
purpose

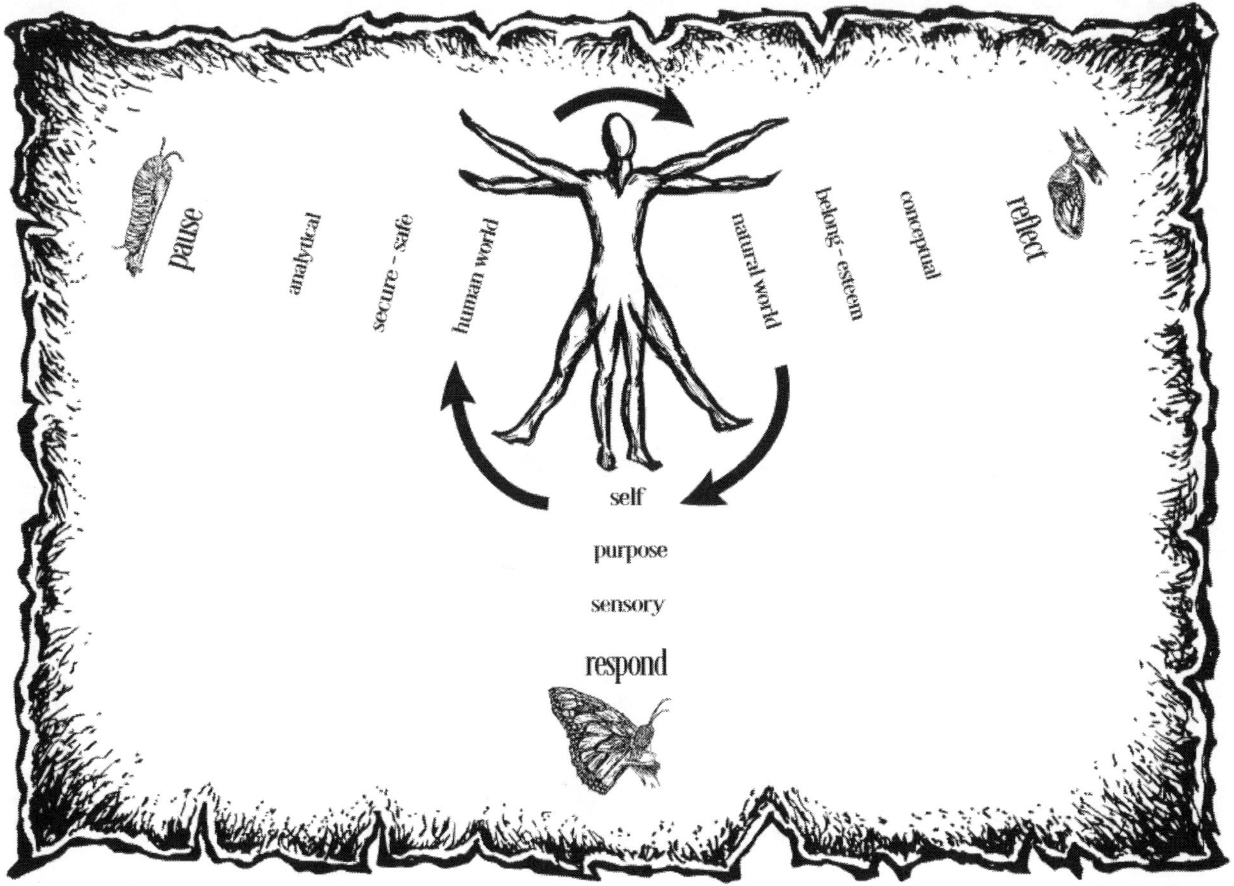

PauseReflectRespond Map | Natural Self Discovery, copyright 2024

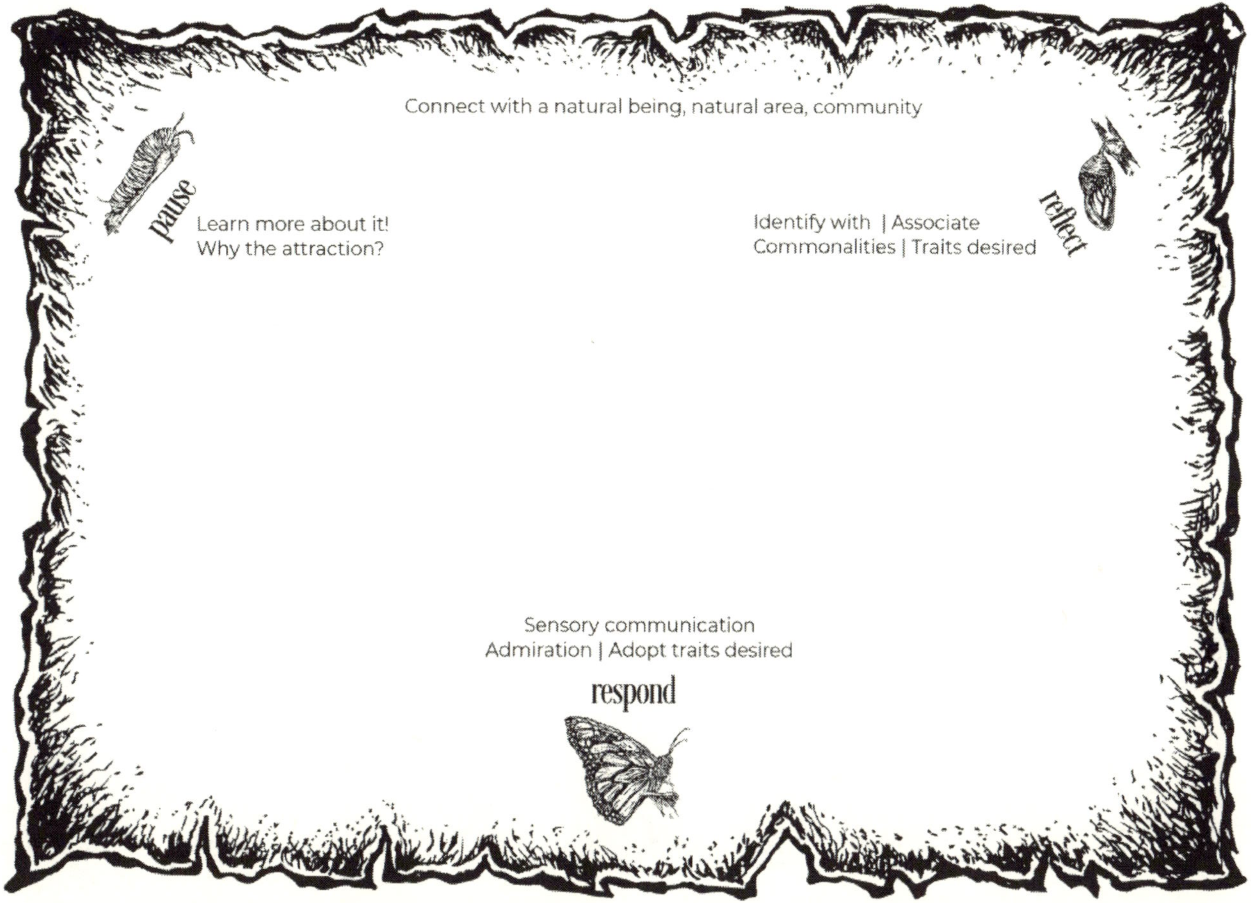
Connect with a natural being, natural area, community
pause
Learn more about it!
Why the attraction?
reflect
Identify with | Associate
Commonalities | Traits desired
Sensory communication
Admiration | Adopt traits desired
respond

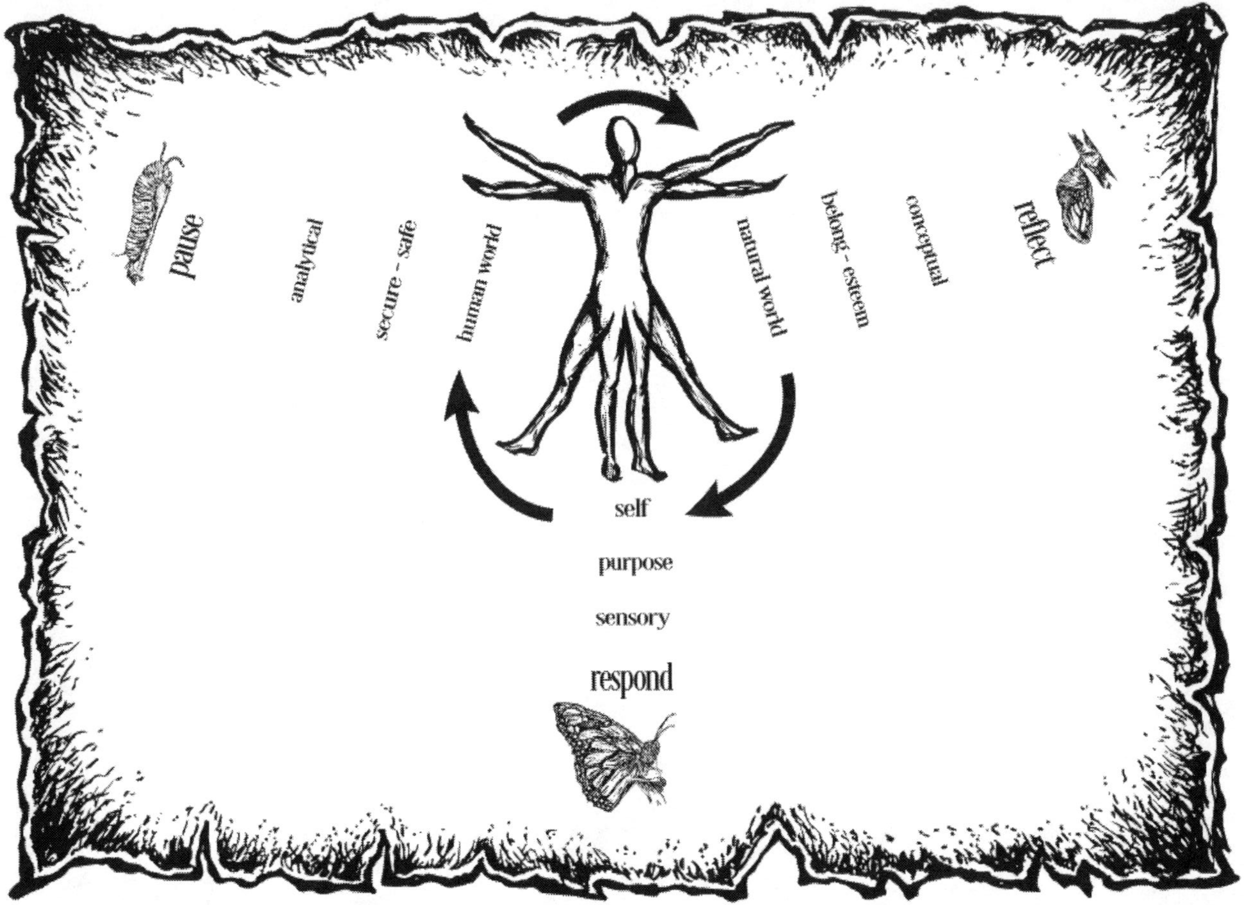

PauseReflectRespond Map | Natural Self Discovery, copyright 2024

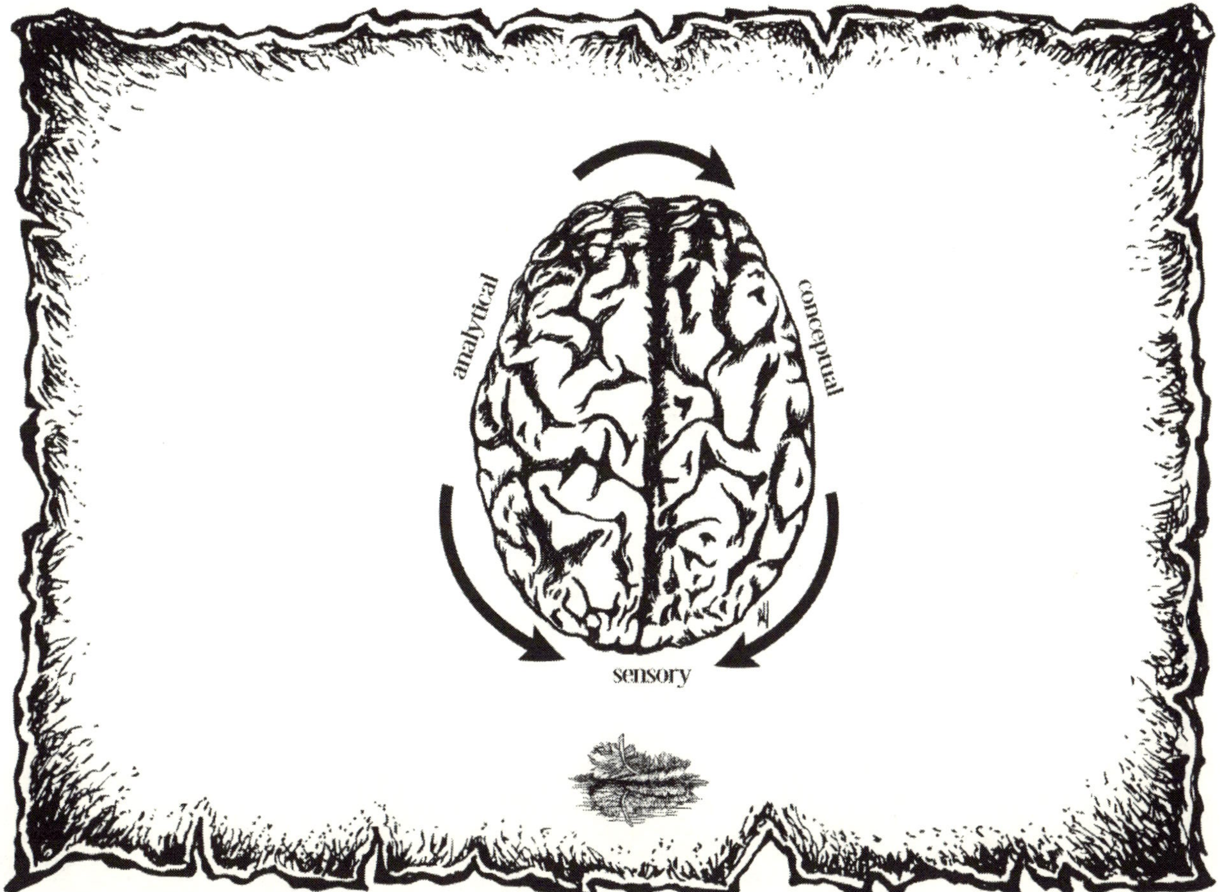
analytical
conceptual
sensory

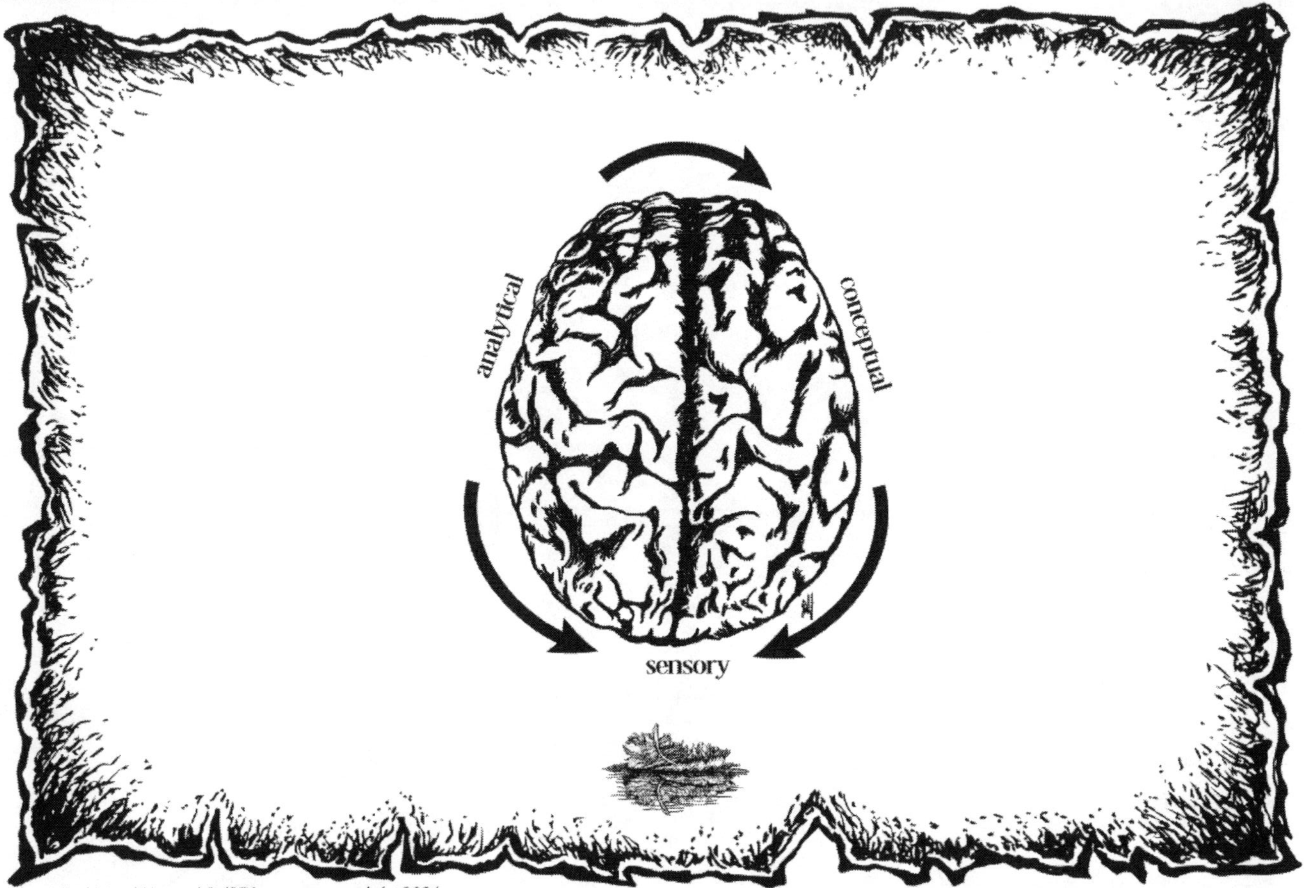
analytical
conceptual
sensory

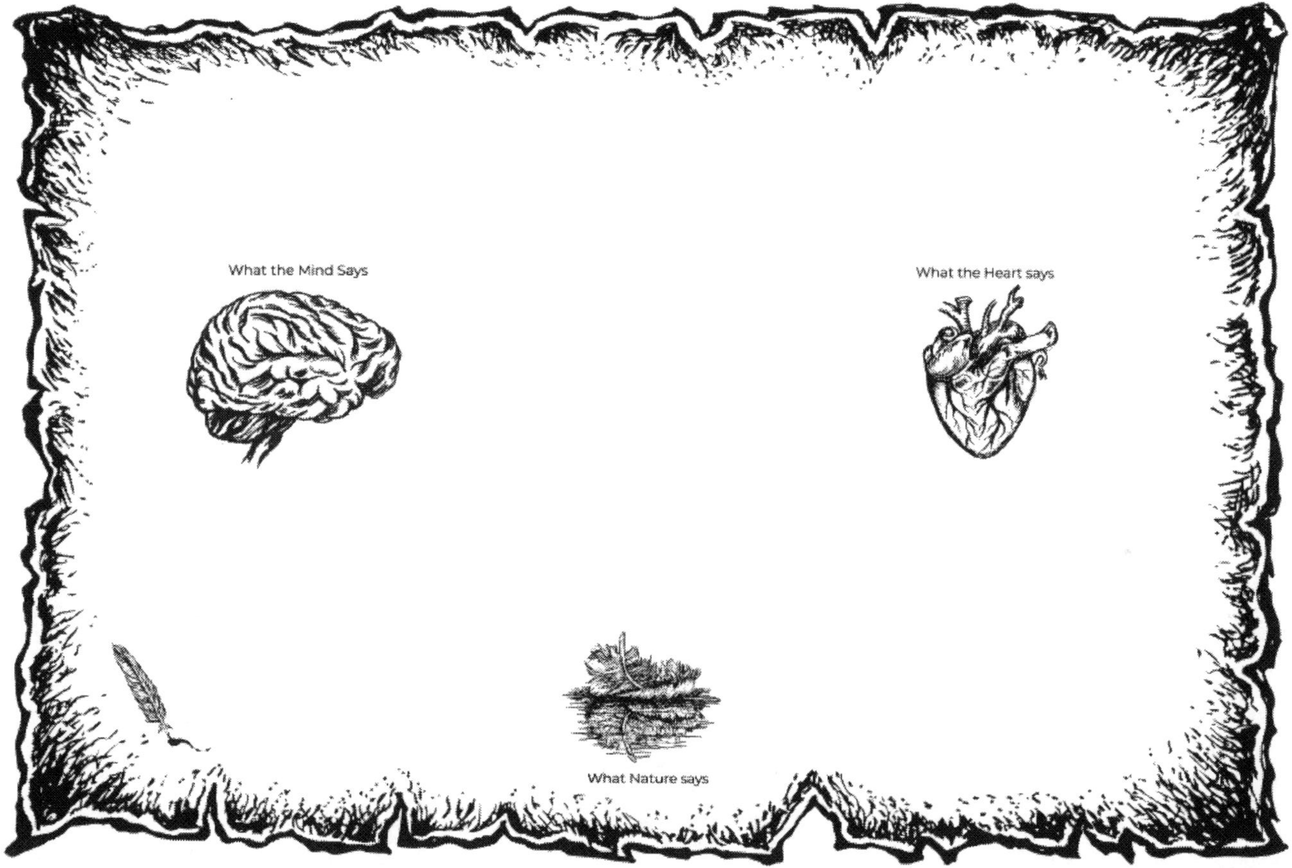

Mind-Heart Trail Map | Natural Self Discovery

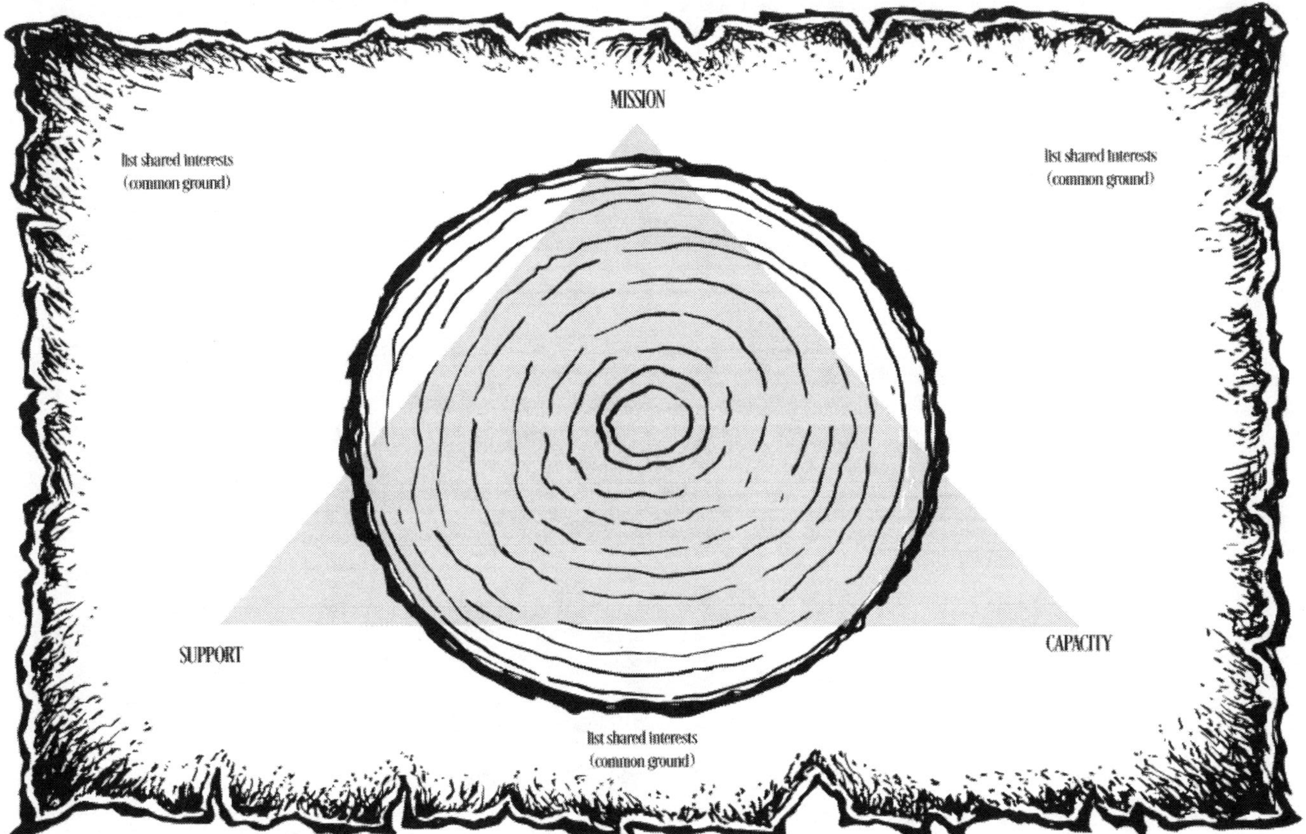

adaption from Dobel/Day Mapping

Natural Alignment Strategy Map | Natural Self Discovery, copyright 2024

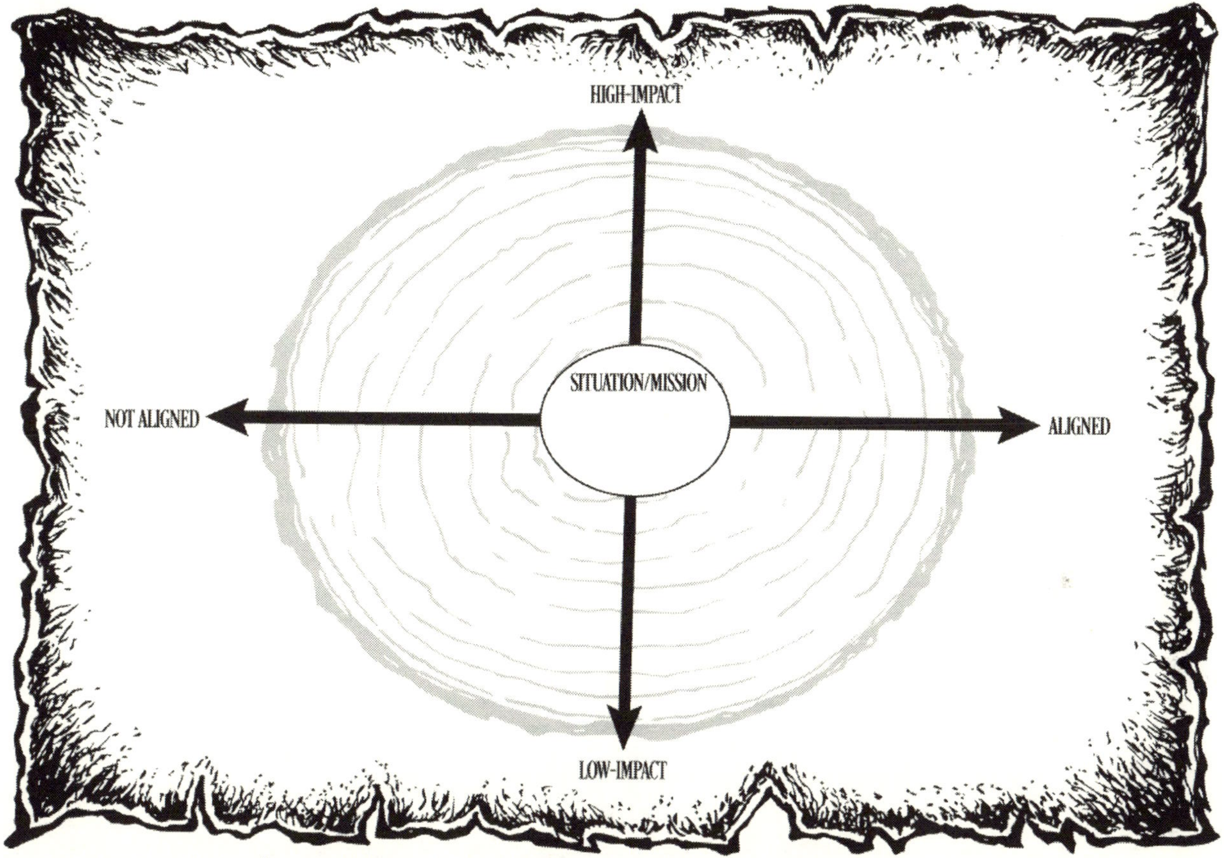

Adapted Forces and Pressures/Power and Influence Map (from Dobel/Day) | Natural Self Discovery, copyright 2024

Learning the universal language of drawing - Everything starts from a simple form, think molecules/cells

drawing is a building process, understanding how things relate, are connected
it is a necessary universal language to learn - it is simply translating what you see & sense, without naming it

daily habit of simple shapes from the natural world - remember, nature doesn't judge!
and allowing time to discover your unique style, it is like your unique fingerprint
just like your handwriting is unique to you
focus on basics shapes, and simple symbols

practice EDGING
every physcial object has an edge, as in,
one sharp side and the fades on another.

practice your style of of adding (gradually building)
VALUES (Shades) and TEXTURE markings to your basic shapes
look for where the darkest darks are, and the lightest lights

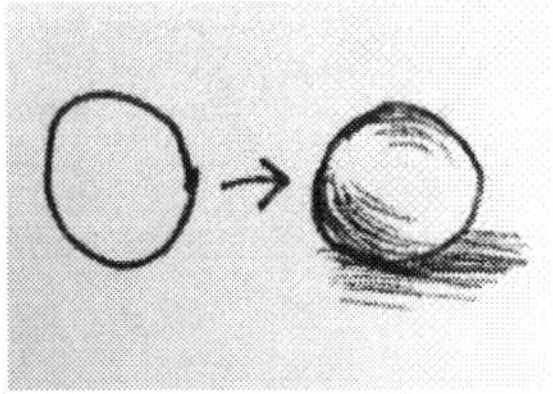

Tips to quiet down your word-side of the brain
focus on how light hits things, and the shapes of that light
look for the simple shapes in everything (ovals, rectangles, triangles), start there lightly, then build from there
if a reference picture, turn it upside down so your right brain is freed up to do it's thing

Left Hemisphere

Analytical thought
Detail Oriented Perception
Ordered Sequencing
Rational Thought
Verbal
Cautious
Planning
Math/Science
Logic
Right Field Vision
Right Side Motor Skills

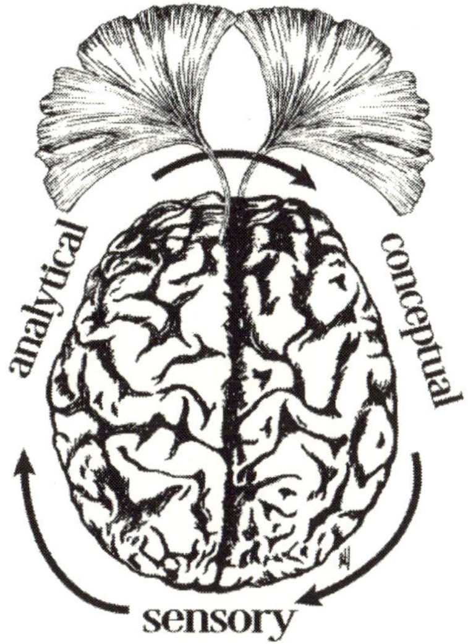

Right Hemisphere

Intuitive Thought
Holistic Perception
Random Sequencing
Emotional Thought
Non-Verbal
Adventurous
Impulse
Creative Writing/Art
Imagination
Left Field Vision
Left Side Motor Skills

A Whole Human Mind Map | Natural Self Discovery, copyright 2024

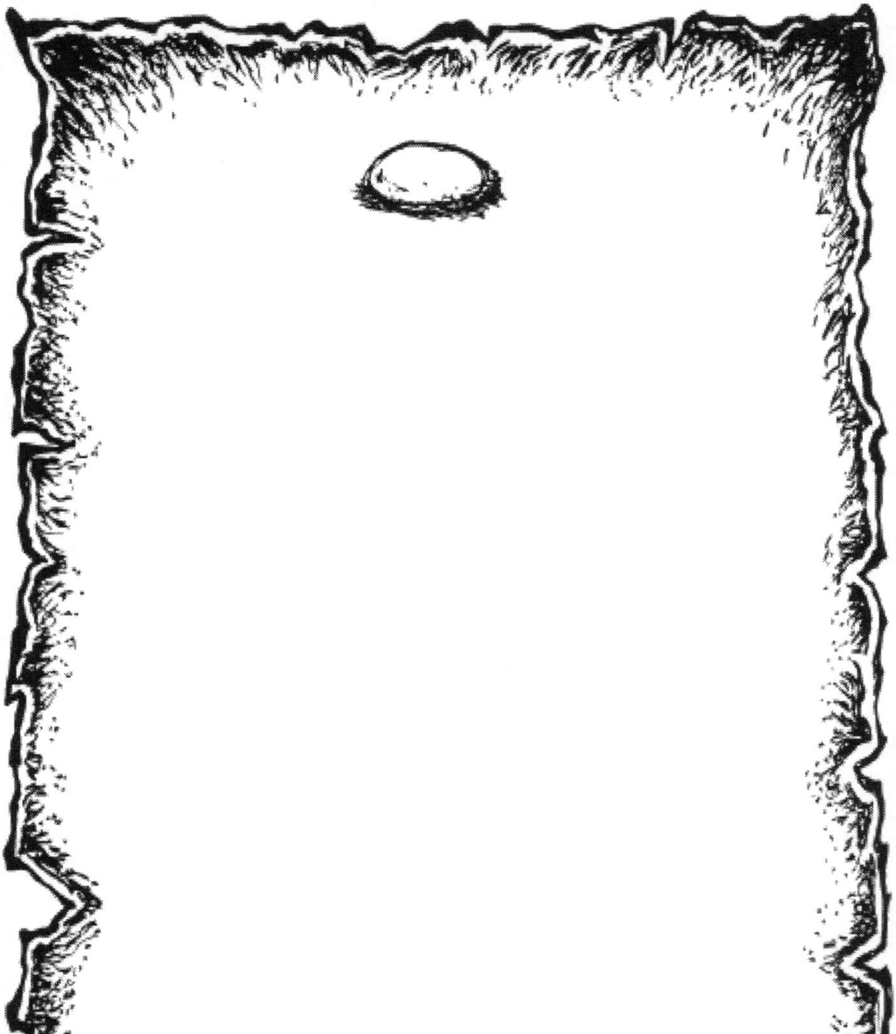

Thought Trail Map | Natural Self Discovery, copyright 2024

just pause
©2024, pamela hoke

Nature Notes...

Nature Notes...

Nature Notes...

Nature Notes...